Retirement Your Way

A practical guide to knowing
what you want and how to get it

Judy Rafferty

Independently Published

First published in 2019

Cover design by Wordsmiths Studio

Printed in the United States
ISBN- 9781693673047

Contents

Introduction...i

Chapter 1.
A promised land: Reinventing the destination.................1

Chapter 2.
Starting with the end: Creating your vision for retirement.................7

Chapter 3.
Checking your map: Turning off the autopilot.................12

Chapter 4.
Retirement fear: Stepping into the void.................17

Chapter 5.
Jumping ship: Deciding whether to retire and when to retire.................22

Chapter 6.
Making a move: Transformation or stagnation?.................29

Chapter 7.
I did it my way: Calling on your experience.................35

Chapter 8.
Finding direction: Getting your time, energy, and interests in sync.....42

Chapter 9.
Mirror, mirror, on the wall: Looking at who you are and who you will be.................47

Chapter 10.
Kicking goals and managing change: Making it happen.................55

Chapter 11.
Signposts along the way: Navigating by your values.................59

Chapter 12.
Invisibility: The relevance deprivation syndrome.................66

Chapter 13.
Relationships and retirement: Looking after each other … and your children 77

Chapter 14.
Dancing to a different tune: Learning new steps 82

Chapter 15.
More new steps: The dance continues 95

Chapter 16.
A bend in the road is not the end of the road: When retirement was not of your choosing 103

Chapter 17.
The happiness hijackers: Depression, anxiety, stress and anger 110

Chapter 18.
Happiness, life satisfaction, and wellbeing: How to make it yours ... 118

Chapter 19.
Fuelling your life: Filling your tanks 127

Chapter 20.
Resizing and relocating: Which way to go? 140

Chapter 21.
Grandparenting: Your next job? 155

Conclusion 164

Introduction

Perhaps you have planned and plotted the retirement phase of your life or perhaps it is unmapped and even unexpected. Maybe your golden years are some way off and you are thinking ahead and learning about retirement so that you will be ready when you exchange your work boots for your golf shoes or your neat black skirt for a comfortable pair of jeans. Regardless of your situation, this book will offer you tools, strategies, and ideas to help you to navigate and optimise this period of your life.

You and I cannot sit together and discuss your reasons for reading this book, nor can you tell me your fears and hopes around retirement. So, I am going to make an assumption. My assumption is that you would like to achieve a retirement that is marked by a sense of purpose and pleasure and leaves little room for regrets. 'Retirement Your Way' will help you to achieve this ideal by providing practical know-how based on my knowledge and many years of experience as a psychology practitioner specialising in helping people transition to retirement. It is a hands-on resource full of activities, tools and information that will enable you to tailor your own retirement with clarity and confidence.

Who is this book for?

For those **considering retirement,** now is the time to start learning about retirement and how to make yours successful. Planning increases the likelihood that you will transit easily and purposefully into this new life phase.

For those **already in retirement**, there is a great deal that you can do to continue to create the retirement you desire and to make it sustainable.

Those who have been **thrust unwillingly into retirement** by life events, such as retrenchment or ill health, have been identified as the most likely to struggle with depression and anxiety. I hope this book will help you to avoid those pitfalls, should you be in this group.

If you have been **working in the home**, perhaps raising a family, or engaged in unpaid community service, this book is also for you. You may not even consider that you are retiring when your duties and engagements change. Certainly, many people will not perceive that you are retiring. This group face retirement issues, such as loss of identity, as their work life changes and becomes less defined. They can also struggle with the need to claim a retirement when it is denied to them by ongoing family demands.

If you are in the group of people who are **struggling to decide whether and when to retire**, this book will help you. You will have a much better understanding of your needs and a sound basis for decision making once you have completed the tasks that will be asked of you.

And finally, the book is written to be a shared **resource for family members or friends** who want to assist the retiring person to transit into this life phase, to meet its challenges, and to retain a sense of worth and purpose.

What this book will offer you

This is a retirement manual. It is full of tasks and questions for you to answer. The activities have been carefully scaffolded so that by the time you have read it you will have a clear idea of:

- what you want in your retirement … a vision
- how to turn the vision into a reality
- how to light the fire in your belly and keep it burning
- your readiness to retire
- how to decide whether and when to retire
- the impact of an involuntary retirement
- how to retain your visibility in an ageist society
- how to synthesise your life's learnings to create two products that you will be proud of: 1) the life you want and 2) the you that you want – a **best** you

- how to maintain your identity
- how to find meaning and purpose
- how to use your experience to make changes
- how to identify and understand depression, anxiety, anger, stress, and grief
- how to protect your relationships in times of change
- how to decide whether to move house, downsize, change locality
- how to walk the line between being a babysitter and a grandparent
- how to deal with the challenges of being a carer-grandparent
- how to protect your happiness
- how to find and grow life satisfaction.

What this book will not offer you

Many people only prepare for this important life phase by considering their financial position. They might ask themselves, 'Can I afford to retire?' If no, then it's back to the grind. If yes, then, 'Great ... I will retire and I will probably travel a lot/go fishing/see more of my children/grand-children ... and I have a few other ideas too'. That might work out, but it is more likely to lead to an initial high followed by a prolonged period of adjustment and confusion.

I am not going to discuss the financial management of retirement. However, I want to encourage you to plan for this aspect of your retirement. Most information on retirement concentrates on financial considerations. It is critical to realistically examine your financial situation prior to retiring. Money does not make us happy, but it does make a difference. An important consideration, that is often not discussed, is expectation. If you expect to have a certain level of financial resource, but you do not achieve it, then your expectation will not be met. Unmet expectation leads to disappointment. Disappointment leads to discontent. In this book we will work to identify your expectations, hopes, and fears about many issues which will assist you to identify the level of financial resourcing you might need in retirement.

How to use this book

Some people read a book from start to finish, others dip and flick. In this book the chapters build upon each other. The tasks in each chapter are designed as a series of steps, but they also stand alone. However, you may wish to go to areas of particular interest to you. This might be the chapter on involuntary retirement or perhaps the chapter on the psychological challenges that can impact on retirement. There are also chapters on specific issues such as downsizing, and grandparenting. If you have an area that is currently challenging, go to that chapter as your priority.

Make sure that you complete each of the tasks in the book. All of the tasks are important. Try not to skip over them even if you feel a task is not relevant to you. I encourage you to have a go at it and assess what you do or don't get from it, and why. Always keep your workings in response to tasks. Some will be used again later in the book and some will be useful for you in the future as you journey through your retirement.

It is very useful to work with another person or a small group. Often, it is the talking around what you have found when completing the tasks that deepens its meaning and value. Do you have a family member, perhaps an adult child, who is not near retirement age but has interest in your retirement journey? I am confident that it would be of significant personal benefit to that adult to undertake, along with you, many of the tasks in the book, and to develop a higher level of self-knowledge. It is of some concern that even middle-aged adults are often unaware of the challenges of retirement. There can be a naivety that asks, 'Why are you worried about not working? I dream of it'. Your expectations, and those of the people around you, will influence the trajectory of your retirement.

Here is your first task.

TASK: Completing the retirement audit

Complete this retirement audit before you begin reading further. I encourage you to complete it again after you have learned all that the coming chapters will reveal to you. It will be interesting for you to compare your before and after results!

Place a cross along the continuum for each factor below.

The extent to which I am looking forward to, or I am currently enjoying, retirement
Low --- **High**

My vision for my retirement is
Undeveloped --- **Developed**

If you are yet to retire … I am confident in making the decision about when to retire
Not at all --- **Very**

If you are yet to retire … I am fearful of retiring and the changes it will bring
Not at all --- **Very**

The expected impact or actual impact of my retirement on my relationships
Low --- **Significant**

My expectation or experience of how retirement will, or does, impact on my relationships
Negative --- **Positive**

My dependence on work (current or not) for my identity and purpose
Nil -- **Significant**

My confidence that my retirement will, or does, match my interests and values
Low --- **High**

My confidence that I will remain useful and interesting as a person in retirement
Low --- **High**

My confidence that my retirement will be, or is, personally rewarding
Low --- **High**

REFLECTION

Note the factors where you have a low score and take special note during chapters that deal with relevant areas.

An invitation

The challenge of retirement is to live it well. It may not be a phase of life that you will have a chance to repeat. It is worthy of an investment of your time and energy to ensure that you do not look back on it with regret but, rather, as a period of time which brought personal contentment and satisfaction and contributed to your wellbeing. This book will provide the means to achieve this. I invite you to turn the page and join me on a journey of self-discovery and self-determination.

Chapter 1.

A promised land: Reinventing the destination

Retirement is a life phase that we may talk about and look forward to with enthusiasm. Yet, at the same time, the thought of retirement may be accompanied by anxiety. It is not unusual to arrive in retirement full of both expectation and trepidation. Reaching retirement can seem bewildering as we quickly discover that, while the Promised Land is indeed full of promise, it requires skilful navigation to avoid the pitfalls – and there is no map.

Should you encounter these pitfalls, they may challenge you at a deep level, asking you to confront and re-evaluate yourself and your life. Retirement raises challenges and asks questions such as:

- What have I achieved in my life so far?
- What has been important to me and will it continue to be important to me?
- How will I continue to have a sense of personal usefulness?
- What will my role be?

The harder you have worked to earn retirement the more invested you might be in your work/career identity. Such an investment can make the transition to retirement more difficult. Don't forget that this also applies to you if you have been working in an unpaid position such as raising children and home making.

Retirement is often bittersweet. Along with the liberation of retirement there seems to be an unspoken caveat. The retirement caveat reads, 'enjoy it, because this is one of your last chances – there is not much life left after this phase'. This caveat can increase the sense of pressure to 'get retirement right'. The information, tasks and the strategies in this book will help you to get it right, to create retirement and life satisfaction and increase your personal wellbeing.

Different roads into the Promised Land

People come to retirement along many different paths. Their stories and their challenges seem quite different, yet I believe that we can address those challenges using similar principles and strategies. Although every situation is unique, most people want quite similar things out of life: connection with others, love and friendship, meaning and purpose, time for self, time to reflect, learning and growth, a clear sense of identity; a life peppered with the highs of happiness and fun, as well as longer-lasting contentment.

Following are stories of people with whom I have worked. Their names have been changed, as have the names of all people mentioned in this book. Notice how their paths to retirement are as diverse as their attitudes, needs, and the challenges that they encountered.

Pauline was 56 when her department was subject to a restructure. Pauline, along with five others, lost her job. This was a difficult time, but she was confident that she would find another position. Two years and no job later she decided that she would officially retire, although she did not want to retire and did not feel ready to do so.

Ed was an easy-going man who just went along with life. At 67 he was not able to keep up with his physically demanding job. He was okay with the idea of retiring but he had not given it much thought. He had started work at the age of 14 and had not been out of work for 53 years. Ed made no plans and was not sure how he would go financially. However, he went well. He had a small house with no mortgage, and he did not have big ideas for his own needs. He had good mates with whom he continued to play cards at night and bowls on weekends. He had a shed with his wood-working gear. He had never married and was used to his own company.

Terry, aged 63, retired after doing substantial preparation. He took two years to structure his finances. He even stopped buying work clothes so that he could wear out the ones he owned. All went according to the detailed plan. But, after he had been retired for six months, his wife, Cynthia, stated that she had been unhappy in their marriage for some years. She told Terry that, now he was home full-time, she could no longer cope. She was going to leave him. Terry's carefully constructed retirement world began to collapse.

Julie went back into the work force when her last child finished school. At the time, Julie was 49. She was very surprised (chuffed, in fact) that she could get back into a retail position after so many years away from it. Now, at age 68, Julie had no intention of retiring, but her husband was anxious to retire. He was keen to finally use the motor home they had invested in some years ago and to indulge in their shared dream of travelling as the whim took them. They shared the dream but the timing was out. Barry was ready. Julie was not. Would Barry retire anyway? Would he do some trips alone? Would Julie give in and retire before she was ready?

Lesley was ready to retire and felt a sense of elation. She had worked hard to rear her children on a single income. She was 65 and had saved hard so that she could afford to care for herself once she was no longer working. Now was to be her time. She spent the months prior to her retirement date looking at possible classes. Drawing, yoga, and patchwork groups were activities she had not had time to participate in fully. Just prior to her leaving work for the last time her second daughter asked her, now that Lesley had time, if she could mind Jamie (aged 3) and Tess (aged 18 months) for three, or maybe four, days a week. 'Not for long,' her daughter assured her, 'just until I can afford to make other arrangements'.

At 48, Barney had it made. He inherited a company from his father. He had been very successful in taking the company from a profitable local enterprise to a national level. He could retire. But did he want to? What would his life look like if he took himself out of his work at an early age?

William had been a magistrate. In the early days he had been proud of his position, but by the time he retired he felt simply satisfied by his career. William was disturbed and embarrassed to find that in his retirement he felt the loss of his title and position, and he wanted to make sure that people knew he had been a magistrate. He often found himself referring to it or bringing it into the conversation.

William's wife, Barb, had never worked – or so she told me with obvious sarcasm. She had raised four children, worked on a variety of committees, cared for both her ageing parents until their deaths, and also for her sister who has a severe mental health disorder. Barb said to me, 'I have retired but no-one seems to notice. My children have left home, my parents have died, and my sister has a paid carer. I am struggling with retirement. And I am struggling with William's retirement'.

Your own path might be similar to those of the people I have just described; or perhaps it is completely different. You might have retired, then returned to work, and are now considering retiring again. Maybe you have cut back on work, a state of not being a full-time worker and not retired. Perhaps you are simply educating yourself in preparation for retirement. No matter how you are currently placed you can enhance what you bring to your life and what your life brings to you.

Redefining retirement

Retirement is a loaded concept and a loaded word. Do we need to retire the word 'retirement'? The word no longer seems to represent the situation well. Retirement as we have understood it is changing. It is unlikely that government-supported pensions for retirement, as we know them, will continue into the future. With increased longevity the idea of retiring at 65 and maintaining our lifestyle for another 20 years is daunting – both emotionally and financially. As individuals facing, or in, retirement, we need to carve a path that leads to enrichment of our own lives. As a society we need the current retirement-focused group to lead us into a new enactment of retirement.

TASK: Renaming retirement

I challenge you to come up with a word or term to replace the word retirement. This is not just a fun task. As you struggle to find a new word or term, I believe it will bring into sharp relief the varied and complex nature of retirement and its changing nature.

REFLECTION

Ask yourself:

- *Does my chosen word convey my sense of retirement?*
- *Does it reflect the currently emerging concept of retirement?*
- *Will it be appropriate to the full range of retirees … those who are retiring very early, because they have achieved success financially or because their health demands it, as well as those who are older and have no choice?*
- *Does it indicate that my time is my own? What about those who have retired but whose time is not their own because of family commitments that now absorb their availability?*
- *Does it mean that you are no longer marching to someone else's drum? What about those who have always been self-employed and in charge of their own time and activity?*
- *Does the word apply to people who officially retire but then continue to work in some capacity or who hold a full-time voluntary position?*

Please let me know if you come up with a winner.

Do we change the word, or do we change the associated meaning of the word? Perhaps it will be the behaviour and actions of this generation, and the ones following closely behind, that will challenge the stereotypes associated with retirement. I would like to think that the word retirement finds a deserved new meaning through action; through YOUR actions in YOUR retirement.

Chapter 2.

Starting with the end: Creating your vision for retirement

Achieving the retirement you want is a personal journey – a journey that allows you to get to know more about yourself and to decide how you will live the next phase of your life. In any journey it is important to have an idea of your destination and a sense of how you will travel there. With a vision and adequate self-knowledge, retirement can become an exciting journey and a rewarding destination.

Do you have a vision for your retirement? Most people, whether retired for years or only considering retiring, have a few ideas and a general sense of what they would like in their retirement, but few have a vision. Creating a vision takes time. It takes self-reflection and self-knowledge. It requires you to know who you are and who you want to be. It necessitates certainty about what you want to stand for in life and what you wish to leave behind when you leave this world. We will be exploring each of these areas in detail as you work through the book, but at this stage you are simply going to begin to create your vision of your ideal retirement.

We all have different ideals and hopes for retirement. There should be no *should* in what you want! In your retirement, you might want to read your way through the local library or catch up on every re-run of the movie classics. Or you might want to climb the Swiss Alps. One is not better than the other. What you want to do will depend in part on your personality. For example, are you an extrovert or an introvert? An extrovert gets energy from being with others, whereas an introvert finds that being with others takes energy. An extrovert's retirement might look quite different from that of an introvert. As well as urging you to be comfortable with your own vision of retirement, I also want to remind you that your retirement vision can change during the experience of retirement. It is understandable if, early in your retirement, you want to sleep, catch up with friends, shop, have coffee, and read the paper. To experience living an unstructured and undemanding life can be as new and different as exploring a foreign country. You may love the new country with its lack of demand and decide to reside there or, as time goes by, you may wish to move on and find a place with more structure and more demanding activity. So, just as in other life phases, what you want and need in your retirement and your vision for your retirement may change over time. This is one reason why it is so important not just to do all the tasks in this book, but to keep them as a record to which you can refer. Perhaps you will redo them when you have a sense that your needs are changing.

Your vision of your retirement

The goal in this chapter is to start the process of creating your vision. I am asking you to think about your retirement and how you want it to be. It is not about how your retirement is currently, if you have already retired. And not as you think it is likely to be, if you are yet to retire. This is a description of how you *want* your retirement to be. As you complete the task don't get stuck because of reality and your constraints. This is about possibilities, about creating a vision.

I am not suggesting that your vision will become a reality. It might – but it is more likely that your vision will become a beacon to guide you and keep you on track. Your vision needs to include many areas of your life. It is not a single goal. If it were, what would happen if you were unable to achieve that goal? Dan told me that he lost his way in retirement after his vision, which was to become a travel writer, failed to become a reality. He retired from his long-held position in an advertising firm with a plan to write travel articles to financially support and add interest to his journeys. He had successfully negotiated a freelance arrangement with a major magazine, and retired full of enthusiasm. Before he could submit his first article the editor of the magazine left, and her replacement told Dan that his services would not be needed. Dan needed to create a more holistic vision – and when he did, he found himself back on track. Retirement is a process, a journey that changes as you travel along its path.

Suzanna wrote her vision and then identified and underlined the important points. It looked like this:

> When I retire next year, I am going to be <u>busy</u> with <u>exercise, friends, family, self-maintenance,</u> and some <u>meaningful work</u> (whether it is <u>paid or not</u>). That work will bring in <u>acknowledgement</u> and it will <u>contribute to my sense of identity</u>. But I will not be bound by it. I will have more time. With that time, I will <u>explore spirituality</u> and other areas for <u>learning</u>. These learnings will give me a <u>reason to travel, to use my skills, to develop new ones, and to feel useful and engaged</u>. I will have a network of <u>old and new friends of all ages</u>, and I will have ways of <u>maintaining and refreshing those connections</u>. I will have a means of expressing <u>creativity</u> and I will <u>share the product</u> of my creativity with others (paid or not). I will be <u>well-dressed</u> and well-groomed. I will keep my <u>brain and body active</u>. I will be in an <u>emotionally sustaining relationship</u> that adds interest and variety and extends me in a healthy and enjoyable way. I will live in a small house but on a block of land big enough for <u>a dog and a garden</u>.

Don't worry at this stage if your vision requires more money than you have. Go for the ideal. Sometimes even entering the land of fantasy is enlightening. Michael wrote that he would fly jets in his retirement. At 68 this was fantasy and Michael happily acknowledged it. However, it started our conversation about how he might get time on a simulator, explore flying lessons or buy a drone.

It is sometimes useful to describe yourself from an outsider's perspective. Imagine you know this person (you) and give a vivid description of him or her. This is the you as you want to be – NOT as you are currently. Go for the ideal, your own personal gold standard.

TASK: Creating a retirement vision

Now it is time for you to start creating your own vision for your retirement by writing, making a mind map or using any other creative idea that appeals to you. Here are some questions to consider:

- *What will you be achieving?*
- *What will you be doing so that you feel useful?*
- *What will you be known for?*
- *What experiences do you want to have?*
- *What have you not yet done that you have always wanted to do?*
- *What will you be doing to have fun?*
- *What will you feel committed to?*
- *Will you be contributing to someone or something in some way?*
- *What are your distinctive qualities?*
- *How will you be spending your day, week, and year?*
- *What does a typical day in your retirement look like?*
- *How will you feel waking up each morning?*
- *How will you look? Dress? Eat?*
- *Where will you be living?*
- *Who will you be sharing your life with?*
- *Will you have an intimate relationship; if so, what will it be like?*
- *What sort of friendships will you have?*
- *How will you treat others?*
- *How will you regard yourself?*
- *How will you be engaging in creativity?*
- *Will you be learning something new?*
- *Will you be developing your current strengths?*
- *What will you regret not doing or trying?*
- *If you had no fear, what would you be doing in your retirement?*

REFLECTION

How did you go? Was it easy for you or difficult? Underline the important points when you are ready. To make those important points come to life you can list them, draw them, create a picture board with magazine cuttings or photos ... be creative.

The creation of a vision takes time and effort, but with a destination in mind you can journey with more certainty. As you progress and your self-knowledge and self-awareness grows, I encourage you to come back and hone this vision. There is very clear evidence that written goals are achieved with far greater frequency than goals which are not specified and written down.

Chapter 3.

Checking your map:
Turning off the autopilot

Retirement is a loaded concept and a loaded word. Do you recall your earlier efforts to try and replace the word 'retirement' with a new word to capture retirement's current and evolving essence? The meaning we give to the word retirement is important. The meaning that you give it will depend on your own history and experience, as well as your cultural beliefs about retirement and ageing.

Not all who retire are old, but retirement is usually directly associated with age, and our society is ageist. Often, we do not value the aged. We imbue age with negativity and, as a result, most people struggle against ageing and anything associated with it: grey hair, wrinkles, forgetfulness. This negativity will affect how we age and how we address the challenges of retirement. Becca Levy, Professor of Public Health and Psychology at the Yale School of Public Health, and other researchers, have shown that negative age stereotypes predict many adverse outcomes among older individuals.[i] Levy's studies have shown that stereotypes influence cognitive and physical performance. People exposed to positive cognitive or physical stereotypes performed significantly better compared to those exposed to negative stereotypes.[ii] Those with more negative age stereotypes demonstrated significantly worse memory performance (a 32% decline) than those with less negative age stereotypes.[iii] One of the highest risk factors for developing Alzheimer's disease is a particular variant of the APOE gene. Those with the gene variant but with positive age beliefs were 49.8% less likely to develop dementia than those with the gene variant and negative age beliefs.[iv]

In a 2012 project sponsored by a partnership under the EU LLP Grundtvig Programme[v], the conclusion was reached that it is very important for people to deal with 'old stereotypes on retirement.' The report also stated that 'almost all seniors need to have a critical look at negative images of ageing and stereotypes on retirement, and replace them with more authentic and empowering images and negative age beliefs'.

This information is probably enough to make you rethink your ideas on ageing and the meaning you give to retirement; but read the results of another study by Levy and her associates. They found that people with more positive self-perceptions of ageing lived, on average, 7.6 years longer than people with more negative views.[vi]

Your beliefs

Are your beliefs and stereotypes about retirement and ageing negative or positive? Are they consistent with your vision for your retirement? Our beliefs are powerful drivers in our lives. They construct for us an internal map which our autopilot will follow unthinkingly unless we become aware and mindful.

As we noted, retirement and age are firmly linked in our minds, so it is important to identify your beliefs with regards to both ageing and retirement. Some beliefs are based on fact; some are based on subjective input such as experience. Factual or not, true or false, these beliefs are difficult to observe or measure objectively or directly. They are the result of learnings and experiences from your own life. As a consequence, your own beliefs can sometimes be difficult to identify.

In addition to being difficult to identify, beliefs can be difficult to separate from fact, especially if they are grounded in childhood. Many beliefs have their roots in the stereotypes learned from elders in childhood or from our life experiences. They may even come from a comment made to you in passing. Often these beliefs are multiple and conflicting. Levy's research has identified the process by which age stereotypes are internalised in younger individuals and then become self-stereotypes when individuals reach old age.[vii]

Following is a list of some of the varied and conflicting responses that others have given when asked to respond spontaneously to the word 'retirement'. Notice how they also include words about ageing.

Answers included: time, freedom, me, watching tv in the middle of the day, loneliness, boring, tracksuits, old people, time to travel, adventure, the next and best part of my life, allowed to be a grumpy old bugger, volunteering, working but not being paid for it, money-poor time-rich, slow drivers, spending the money I have worked so hard for, time for coffee and friends, time to get my health and body back, finding time for my painting at last, getting close to the end of life.

Marty struggled with a conflict of beliefs. He said, 'I recall saying that, while I did not want to get old, there would be some good things about it, like retirement. I believed I would be able to do anything I liked when I liked, especially sitting in the sun and reading. I recall mentioning that I would be able to eat anything I liked because it would not matter if I put on a bit weight. I am not prepared to disclose how old I was when I expressed such naïve thoughts, but, silly as it sounds, I used to think like that. And, to be honest, a part of me still believes that retirement is a time when I can stop trying hard and, instead, do what I like. But another part of me won't let this happen. I could not let myself go. I know I won't stop trying just because I have retired – at least, I hope I won't'.

It is important to be able to separate your desire for your own retirement from your underlying beliefs. Otherwise those beliefs may trip you up as you navigate towards your vision of retirement.

Your internal maps for retirement

Your internal maps are largely subconscious and are founded on your internalised beliefs. Your autopilot follows these maps. To uncover your internal maps for retirement you will need to examine the thoughts and images that come to mind when I ask you to think about retirement. Having viewed many responses to this request, it is clear to me that individuals tend to have multiple – and often conflicting – beliefs about retirement. It is also apparent that frequently people have an internalised view of retirement that is somewhat negative and ageist which is at odds with another, more optimistic, view that they have structured for themselves and about themselves. One man wrote of retirement:

... time to do what I want. I don't want to be like my dad and his mates. They retired and did nothing for the next 20 years. I won't be doing that. In fact, to tell you the truth, the idea of doing nothing much for years scares me. I see myself as doing all the things I have not yet done in life.

TASK: Uncovering your internalised beliefs about retirement and ageing

Write the word RETIREMENT at the top of your page. Jot down all the words and thoughts that come to mind in response to this word. Next, write the word RETIREE and again jot down all the words and thoughts that come to mind. Finally, do this again for the words OLD PERSON.

REFLECTION

Go back to your vision of retirement that you wrote about in Chapter 2: Starting with the end.

- *Do your internal beliefs about retirement and ageing support the vision of retirement which you created in Chapter 2? Is there consistency between the two?*
- *Is there anything you need to do differently in order to align your retirement vision and your internal map of retirement?*

A healthy, vibrant retirement is a critical factor in successful ageing. And healthy, vibrant ageing is a critical factor in a successful retirement.

[i] Levy, B.R., Ferrucci, L., Zonderman, A.B., Slade, M.D., & Resnick, S.M. (2016). 'A culture-brain link: Negative age stereotypes predict Alzheimer's disease biomarkers.' *Psychology and Aging.* 31(1), 82-88. doi: 10.1037/pag0000062.

[ii] Levy, B. (2003). 'Mind matters: Cognitive and physical effects of aging self-stereotypes.' *The Journals of Gerontology, Series B: Psychological Sciences and Social Sciences.* 58(4), 203-211.

[iii] Levy, B.R., Zonderman, A.B., Slade, M.D., & Ferrucci, L. (2012). 'Memory shaped by age stereotypes over time.' *The Journals of Gerontology, Series B: Psychological Sciences and Social Sciences.* 67(4), 432-436. doi: 10.1093/geronb/gbr120.

[iv] Levy, B.R., Slade, M.D., Pietrzak, R.H., & Ferrucci, L. (2018). 'Positive age beliefs protect against dementia even among elders with high-risk gene.' *PLOS ONE.* 13(2). doi: 10.1371/journal.pone.0191004.

[v] GRUNDTVIG Lifelong Learning Programme. (2012). *Pre-retirement counselling: A shortcut to active ageing.* Retrieved from: https://transitionsinlaterlife.files.wordpress.com/2014/10/final-report-senior-career-counselling.pdf.

[vi] Levy, B.R., Slade, M.D., Kunkel, S.R., & Kasl, S.V. (2002). 'Longevity increased by positive self-perceptions of aging.' *Journal of Personality and Social Psychology.* 83(2), 261-270.

[vii] Levy, B.R. (2003). 'Mind matters: Cognitive and physical effects of aging self-stereotypes.' *The Journals of Gerontology, Series B: Psychological Sciences and Social Sciences.* 58(4), 203-211.

Chapter 4.

Retirement fear:
Stepping into the void

You have created your own vision for your retirement and examined your beliefs about retirement. So now, let's address the fear that can challenge your vision, cause you to postpone retirement or not step fully into the retirement you are currently living. Many people fear retirement. Fortunately, while there is a basis for retirement fear, there is also a solution — and you are reading it right now! The research shows that pre-retirement education that extends beyond financial planning is associated with post-retirement wellbeing. If you have already retired, it is not too late to undertake further education and planning.

A survey among retired persons in the USA showed that of all the major changes and transitions in a lifetime, such as getting married, having children, children leaving the home etc. — a majority of 41% found retirement the most difficult.[i] Retirement is life changing. It can feel like you are exchanging certainty for risk, the known for the unknown. The unknown is always a little scary, even if it is a positive fear. Will your lifestyle change when you have less money coming in, will your relationship change for better or worse, who will you be, what will you be doing? Often it is this last question that fans retirement fear and leads people to postpone retirement. Margaret is a calm and thoughtful woman, who had to retire early due to ill health. She told me that she was not prepared for the emptiness she found, particularly in the early days, of her retirement. When Margaret spoke to me about it, she called it the void.

The void

The void is the empty space in your life created by the absence
of work. As you try to peer into the future, do you see a void?
When you are not working, what will you be doing? For those
who have already retired, sometimes the void can open up
unexpectedly as the rush of doing all the things work did not
permit eases to a trickle. Some try to protect themselves
against the void by filling life with plans and activities. Voids
can occur suddenly or loom towards you. They can occur and
pass within an hour or a day or they can last much longer and
feel as if you will be trapped for the rest of your life. The void
seems to be one of the biggest non-financial causes of anxiety
for people facing, or in, retirement.

Not everyone will fear the void. For some, it is a familiar
space. For others, the lack of commitment suits their personality. However, for many people it is a dauntingly empty
space. We tend to equate busyness with success and importance. And while we might resent it, work provides busyness. As a society we seem to strive to fill every possible void.
'Avoid a void' might be a guiding principle of this current era.

When Gareth retired, he decided to take a minimum of six
months to, in his words, 'just be'. He had been self-employed
from the age of 22. By the age of 65, he was employing staff
to run rental properties, a laundromat, a cleaning service, and
a bed and breakfast. His work was more than full-time. Early
in his six months of sitting in the void, his concerned son said
to him, 'What's the matter with you? It's not like you to be
doing nothing. Perhaps you are depressed'. Smiling, he told
his son, 'I am not doing nothing, although it might look that
way after 43 years of busyness. I am busy in a different way. I
am learning to be with myself again'. I suggested to Gareth
that perhaps he was in the void. He agreed and said, 'I am
stepping into the void to see what's really there. Maybe I will
find another part of myself. Maybe I will find another way to
be in the world'.

Learning to be with yourself, without the distraction – and
reward – of work, can be difficult. Some months after our first

discussion I asked Gareth more about his experience of learning to be with himself, learning to be in the world in a different way and about what he was finding in the void.

Turning the void into a vacancy

'Firstly,' said Gareth, 'I have had to develop trust. Trust that I am worth being with, trust that the void is a friendly place which will offer me something. Trust that the void will be a good place for me to meet with myself.' He went on to explain, 'I have always had a dislike of not using time well. Maybe I dislike it because I actually fear wasting time and missing opportunities. What do the kids call it now? FOMO – fear of missing out. When I was working and I had a day with no plans, I felt relief. It was a well-earned and time-limited experience. Nowadays when I see a day ahead with no plans, an empty day, I start to feel an emptiness in me. Is it boredom? Is it loneliness? It cannot be either, because at that stage I am only aware of the day ahead. I am not experiencing boredom or loneliness. I am anticipating it. And then I want to fill up the day and get busy. However, I assure myself that the emptiness is not an empty void, but a space; a vacancy, if you will. One I can choose to fill, or not. Just like one of my rental properties. I can leave the place empty, I can move in myself, I can put friends in, or I can put in people who I don't know and I don't want to know, and make money instead. These days I am giving myself the choice.'

Michael Leunig[ii] writes:

> *Come sit down beside me, I said to myself.*
> *And although it didn't make any sense,*
> *I held my own hand as a small sign of trust*
> *And together I sat on the fence.*

Take it easy

Longhurst, in his research, found that it takes up to five years for people to make the transition to retirement.[iii] Take your time to turn the void into a vacancy. If you feel fear, anxiety or discomfort as you face the unknown, allow yourself to feel it and step into the void regardless. It is not a big black hole that will swallow you. It is a period of time that WILL pass. Try not to fill it just to avoid it. Assure yourself it has something to offer you, a place to be with yourself. Unless you can spend time with yourself, you are in danger of missing your own life.

TASK: Stepping into the void

Complete one of the following statements. Write spontaneously and at any length.

I have no fear of a void because …

....

....

....

I fear the void because …

....

....

....

REFLECTION:

Consider how your fear, or lack of fear, might influence your retirement.

---

[i] GRUNDTVIG Lifelong Learning Programme. (2012). *Pre-retirement counselling: A shortcut to active ageing.* Retrieved from: https://transitionsinlaterlife.files.wordpress.com/2014/10/final-report-senior-career-counselling.pdf.

[ii] Leunig, M. (2014). 'Come sit down beside me.' *Boyle poetry*. Retrieved from https://russellboyle.word-press.com/2014/07/17/come-sit-down-beside-me-by-michael-leunig/.
[iii] Longhurst, M. (2018). Enjoying retirement: An Australian handbook of ideas, strategies and resources. Sydney:Hachette Australia.

Chapter 5.

Jumping ship:
Deciding whether to retire
and when to retire

This chapter will be of special interest to readers who have yet to retire. However, I believe there is benefit to be gained by reading this chapter even if you have already jumped ship.

Deciding to retire can feel like abandoning the ship of plenty and throwing yourself into uncharted waters. The ship of plenty has provided you with money, purpose and sometimes even prestige, or at least a sense of competence and identity. But passage on this ship comes at a cost. You have paid with your time and your energy – in fact, with the years of your life. There may come a time when you no longer want to pay this price, when the benefits seem less than the cost, when it feels like the ride is over. When this happens, you will begin to consider whether it is time to retire. Not everyone can make a choice about whether or not to retire. Many of us are compelled to continue to work, usually for financial reasons. And some people are forced into retirement.

If you do have a choice, then it is often a hard decision to make. Do you prioritise income and the lifestyle and opportunities associated with that income? Or do you create a new lifestyle that was previously unavailable because of work commitments? How do you balance the seesawing between time and money? Unknowable factors may make the decision to retire seem like a gamble. The unknowable factors include how long you will live, whether you will enjoy the benefits of not working more than the benefits of working, how much money you will need, and how much your nearest and dearest might need in terms of financial assistance and your time and practical support. Many people swing between two worries.

Worry 1

What if I decide to postpone retirement in order to fill up the coffers, but run out of good health and the opportunity to enjoy the money and leisure after years of working?

Worry 2

What if I decide to retire and enjoy my life before I run out of good health and mobility, but then I run out of money?

It is daunting to think of a time when we are no longer working and there is no money coming in, except from investments or a pension, to support our wants and needs. And it is daunting to suddenly become a non-worker because, as we know, work provides more than just money. It can provide many secondary gains such as purpose, structure, self-esteem, and social contact.

Despite the good things that work provides for us, it seems that many people reach a point where they want a change. There is an internal drive to stop, to do something differently. This is not the case for everyone. Doug told me that he will never stop working and that he cannot understand the need to stop. Doug is now 72 and he intends to work until he dies. On the other hand, Glenn explained to me that he is happy enough at work but that, at the age of 56, he has started to think increasingly about giving it up and either retiring or doing something else. In my experience, more people are like Glenn than Doug. I realise that I am making a generalisation, but it seems that at some time, usually after the age of 50, a shift in thinking slowly begins to emerge. There is a lessening of career drive, and a quietly growing interest in change or difference. It may be as simple as a need to challenge or find the self in another forum; for example, learning to ride a motor bike, creating a garden or doing a gruelling mountain walk in a foreign land.

As individuals move towards their late 50s and early 60s the balance between engagement in work and non-work often begins to shift. Absorption in, and planning around, work lessens. It is as though the person becomes distracted. Consider your own experience with being absorbed in an activity such as reading a good book or working on a task that requires your focus and attention. Despite your absorption, your attention finally starts to wander. You become aware of sounds or movement nearby. You stretch and look away. Something takes your attention. Perhaps it is a task that needs to be done, or the coffee machine sitting on the bench, or the sunny day outside. You might try going back to the activity or the book, and continue to work or read, but you tend to find that your attention wanders increasingly until you stop what you are doing and move on. This is not dissimilar to what happens when we begin to withdraw from work. It is not necessarily a plan. It can just happen.

It is in this period, planned or unplanned, that we may begin to start to think about retirement and ask ourselves questions such as:

- Should I retire?
- Should I change jobs?
- Should I do something completely different?
- Should I do the same job part-time?
- Should I take an extended holiday?
- Can I afford to change jobs/work less/retire?

TASK: Answering the difficult questions of retirement timing

Consider the following:

- *Why am I thinking about making a change?*
- *Has something changed in either myself or my life that is prompting me to consider a change?*
- *Will a leave of absence restore me? What evidence and experience do I have to suggest that it will or will not? Am I able to take extended leave and then reassess?*
- *Does my financial state determine what I can do? Have I sought expert advice on my financial situation?*
- *If I do/do not make a change, how will I feel about myself in five years' time?*

REFLECTION

Use your answers to help you begin to identify your next step. Do you need to source financial advice? Might you explore taking time off? Would you benefit from making an online search of the current job market? Undoubtedly, a next step includes reading this book and completing the work contained within it. Once you have done this you will have a very good understanding of your level of preparation for retirement and what more you need to do in order to be better prepared. Whether you move directly into retirement or whether you get there through stepped phases, such as reduced hours, it is beneficial to prepare.

New ways to retire

Earlier we mentioned two worries that are common to people deciding to retire. They are: 'What if I decide to postpone retirement in order to fill up the coffers, but run out of good health and the opportunity to enjoy the money and leisure after years of work?' and 'What if I decide to retire and enjoy my life before I run out of good health and mobility, but then I run out of money?'

Perhaps these worries come from a definition of retirement that is about working/not working. In the working/not working understanding of retirement we have life periods that are identified as:

Work life: a long period of activity directed towards funding life's requirements and, if possible, building a financial reserve.

Retirement life: a final period of using financial reserves to fund life's requirements while not working.

Deciding to retire is no longer a dichotomous dilemma, an either-or decision between working and not working. In *Chapter 1: A promised land*, you tried to come up with a new word for the retirement phase of life and we talked about changing the enactment of retirement. Many people want to continue to work in some capacity in their retirement – paid or not.

We might re-conceptualise retirement as retiring ONLY from being oriented to the wealth-growing life phase through the process of labour, rather than necessarily retiring from work. This is an attitudinal change. A subtle, but important, fear-reducing difference.

Pre-retirement

If the step into retirement feels too big, then break it down into smaller steps. You can do this by easing your work load. Going part-time is a great way to step into retirement. It is not always an option, but increasingly there are jobs that will allow it.

If you work part-time, it will give you the opportunity to do a dry run. You can trial living on less income. You can trial the activities that you believe may give you pleasure in retirement. You can test your capability in the art and discipline of living without an external structure to organise you. You can begin learning to balance the seesaw of doing too much and not doing enough. Some people in retirement find that they have too little to do. Some people find that they take on too much and end up overloaded with activities and commitments. Most people take some years to get it 'just right'.

Are you able to think of new enactments and novel paths into retirement? Here is one idea – when the urge to stop work grows insistent, perhaps consider stopping earlier than you might otherwise do. But stop with an intention to return. This is not just an extended holiday. It is a retirement of some years' duration followed by a return to work. Increasingly, I am suggesting this option and increasingly, people are actioning it.

Ian and Paula were in their late 50s. Both worked long hours. They said that they were desperate to retire but had a plan to 'stick it out' for another five to seven years. Fit and full of energy, they were using annual holidays to travel adventurously. I suggested to them that they retire now for the five-to-seven-year period and then in their mid-60s re-enter the work force. Initially they found it difficult to consider this as a real possibility. However, they listened as I explained why *now* could be the time to act. They were burnt out and wanting to be elsewhere, but they were fit and healthy. Their retirement ideas included more overseas travel, more kayaking and camping trips locally, and building an eco-sustainable flat in their garden that could be rented and become an extra income source – all activities which require energy and health.

Often work seems like a burden in our 50s and 60s, but a privilege as we move into our 70s and beyond. Coming back into the workforce later in life can provide excitement and stimulation. It can offer a boost to self-esteem. And, of course, it helps to refill financial resources. It can be easier to spend money when you know that the income stream has only paused, not stopped. A consideration when evaluating this option is whether your type of job (or skill) will still be available to you if you have not been practising it for some time.

It was easy for Paula, who was an experienced administrator in a private school. She was confident that she would be able to find work again. Ian was an accountant and felt it would not be possible to catch up again, should he take time off. However, he decided that if he limited his practice to income tax return preparation it should be manageable. He thought he would try to find work as an employee rather than having the burden of running his own practice. Perhaps he might also be able to work at peak tax times and not work during the quiet periods. Paula and Ian are three years into their 'retirement' and enjoying it. They have not put a date on their final retirement, but they know, because they have learned the skills of retirement, that it will be a simple decision to make in the future. Remember there is no one-size-fits-all answer to the questions of whether and when to retire. Try to brainstorm new pathways into retirement, preferably with friends who are also reading this book. My recipe for stimulating creativity and activating lateral thinking includes the careful mixing of good food and good wines.

Chapter 6.

Making a move: Transformation or stagnation?

Once you have made the decision to retire you will enter into transition. In psychology, a transition is the process of moving from one state of being to another. If we break life up into phases, then it becomes clear that there will be a transition between each phase. Transition is a process that takes time. It is the time taken to transit between two phases in your life … the time it takes to let go of your investment in one phase and to reinvest in, and identify yourself with, another phase. Transition time can be long or short. It can be obvious or only apparent in retrospect. Sometimes, it feels that the transition is like a long and winding road between the phases. At other times, it seems as if the phases butt up against each other with no road between.

I have worked with many people experiencing transition. The work of William Bridges[i], in his book *Managing transitions: Making the most of change*, stimulated my thinking in this area. Bridges is an internationally recognised figure in organisational change management. He developed a model of transition that suggests that personal transitions start with an ending, progress through a neutral zone, and finish with a new beginning. Bridges describes a process with which most psychologists are now familiar, although this may not have been the case when the book was first published in 1991. Despite its age, it is a book that is still worth reading.

My way of thinking is similar to that of Bridges, and to currently accepted wisdom. In my model of transition there are six steps:

1. Contemplation
2. A change
3. An ending
4. Connecting time
5. A transformation
6. A beginning.

Step 1 – Contemplation

Contemplation is thinking without acting. You may be thinking about retirement and considering your options but are yet to take action. This step may be missed if your retirement was not your decision.

Step 2 – A change

This step usually starts with a change that happens in either our external or internal world. We change jobs. We change partners. We have a car accident that causes us permanent damage. We lose interest in what we have been doing for the last 20 years. Our priorities change. We become grandparents. Too many friends die.

The change can be something we choose or simply something that happens to us. My experience is that many people come to retirement before they intended because something changes inside of them. There is a shift from wanting to earn money and to be a good XYZ (fill in job title) to wanting to do something new, perhaps to contribute and to do something that matters ... something that makes a difference.

Step 3 – An ending

This ending happens in our internal world. The change experienced in Step 2 sets off an internal struggle that ends our relationship with ourselves and our internal world as we have known it to date. If, as happens in retirement, our role in the world is unplugged and if our identity is disrupted, then we have come, ready or not, to an ending.

Step 4 – Connecting time

Connecting time is the time between the ending and the transformation. We do not have to take the road to transformation. Some people determinedly stay put, refusing to take the journey into the unknown. Without transiting beyond Step 3 there is no transformation; and when there is no transformation there is a danger of stagnation.

Connecting time is often lonely, confusing, and difficult. It is scary and there is no map, nor any indication of how long it will take you to arrive at your destination. While you are walking along the unmapped road you may feel that you are uncertainly wandering and wondering. But when you have safely arrived you will look back on this stage as the time of connection between the old you and the new you, between your old life and your new life.

Step 5 – A transformation

In Step 5 you enter into transformation. It can be liberating and renewing. It may feel exciting. Transformation is more than change. It is an internal experience, a shift – perhaps in how you see yourself or your life. It is the energy and relief of transformation that provides the impetus to undertake Step 6 – a new beginning and all that it entails.

Step 6 – A beginning

Beginnings usually come with both excitement and anxiety. They hold an element of the unknown and unknowable. A beginning requires initiative and takes some energy. However, the power of transformation can carry you through this process.

As you read the description of transition you may find yourself thinking, 'I am only going to retire, not transform into some new creature!' Some people go into retirement without a flicker of concern or drama. For others it is transformative and therefore difficult. The difference may lie in your level of psychological readiness.

In retirement you will undoubtedly experience Step 2. There has to be change in your internal or external world. Even if you minimise the change (for example, you might plan to go on long service leave for 12 months and then slip seamlessly into retirement), there will still be a big change from being an employed person on holidays to someone who is no longer employed.

When you move into retirement you will also experience Step 3, an end. The ending may be softened if you have a rewarding voluntary job lined up or you are going to continue to do some casual or consulting work.

If Step 3 is softened to the degree that you do not need to find a new role or struggle with identity then Step 4, connecting time, may be avoided altogether. You may slip easily into retirement. If not, and if your retirement was sudden and unplanned, you may find yourself immersed in Step 4 and wondering why you feel so disconnected and disinterested, so empty and confused. But take heart – this is a powerful time in your life which can lead to great rewards. The reward is transformation of you and your life. You will come out of the darkness into a life that is truly your own and a self whom you know and recognise. And once there, you can begin your new phase of life with confidence.

Transitions are an important part of human development and growth, regardless of which century and which culture we live in. The critical element of a transition is that it takes time and it happens away from our family and friends; usually in emotional isolation. It can be painful and frightening, and there is no sure outcome. We know that other cultures have initiation ceremonies. These are stories of transition. We have many fairy tales that are really stories of transition. As an example, think about the fairy tale Rapunzel.

Rapunzel lived a safe, but limited, life in a tower:

- Step 1. Rapunzel looks out from her tower window and considers her life – contemplation.
- Step 2. The prince arrives in Rapunzel's life – change in external world.

- Step 3. Rapunzel falls in love and wants a new role as the prince's wife – end of herself and her role in life as she has known it.
- Step 4. Rapunzel escapes the tower to live in the wilderness alone, to wonder and to wander – connecting time.
- Step 5. Rapunzel finds her prince. Rapunzel is free and the prince's sight is restored – transformation for each.
- Step 6. Rapunzel and the prince marry and start their lives together – a beginning.

While I have proposed a model and applied it to retirement, it is, like most models, inadequate to meet the entire range of human experiences and you may struggle to apply it to yourself. For some people the steps are sometimes only apparent in retrospect or they appear to occur out of order. For example, a person can apparently miss the wandering and wondering of Step 4 (connecting time) and travel directly into Step 6 (a beginning). But this pseudo beginning may really be part of Step 2 (a change), with the excitement of freedom and unstructured time. In this situation, as Steps 3 (an ending) and 4 (connecting time) emerge, you may feel confusion and disappointment and question the wisdom of your retiring. In trying to understand your own confusion you may decide, for example, that the problem is not with your retirement, but with your spouse of 30 years or with the town where you live. Understanding the process of transitions can help you to avoid these anxieties and pitfalls.

TASK: Where are you on the road to retirement?

Circle one of the following steps:

Step 1	*Contemplation*	*Step 4*	*Connecting time*
Step 2	*A change*	*Step 5*	*Transformation*
Step 3	*An ending*	*Step 6*	*A beginning*

REFLECTION

- *What are you experiencing that has led you to identify you are at this step?*
- *Is something holding you back from moving to the next step?*
- *What will move you to the next step?*

---

[i] Bridges, W. (1991). *Managing Transitions: Making the most of change.* Reading, Mass: Addison-Wesley.

Chapter 7.

I did it my way:
Calling on your experience

Now that you understand the process and structure of transition, let's explore the skills you already have for stepping through this challenging time. By entering retirement, you are ending your work phase. Even if you are still doing some work, you are ending the phase where work is primary. And endings come with loss. Do I hear you snigger? 'What loss?' you might say, 'loss of having to get up each morning according to an alarm clock, loss of having to hurry to catch the bus, loss of five days a week that I cannot call my own?' And I reply, 'What about loss of income, identity, purpose, structure?'

Transition is challenging regardless of whether you have chosen to enter a new phase or it has been thrust upon you. A transition is usually easier if it is a chosen path. Typically, if you have chosen the path then you will let go of your last staging post more easily. If you have been thrust onto the path, you may be more likely to cling to the old and resent the new. It is also easier if, having chosen the path, you have an idea of your destination and you have a road map with you. But it is not necessary. In fact, I would suggest that, while easier, having a prescribed destination and a set of plans and directions is not the best approach. It may mean that you do not fully utilise the opportunity for growth and transformation. Joseph Campbell, an American writer and orator, is accredited with saying, 'If you can see your path laid out in front of you step by step, you know it's not your path. Your own path you make with every step you take. That's why it's your path'.[i]

Experience counts in making transitions ... A company asked me to provide a consultancy when they laid off quite a few workers. I interviewed all of those who lost their job. Some were understandably distraught and fearful of the future. Others were angry with the company. But a few were calm and accepting. These last few people had all experienced a previous significant career change that was out of their control. For one, this was his third redundancy. Another had had to change from being self-employed to becoming an employee when he lost all his own equipment in a flood; and one had to find a new career after she sustained a hand injury. These people had their previous experience of transition to call upon. It meant that they felt some certainty about the difficulties ahead and how they would map and navigate those challenges.

Transition skills

Your transition skills will be unique to you. However, there are some important skills that work well for everyone. One is to be able to tolerate uncertainty. Uncertainty is uncomfortable. It is nice to know what to expect and what you are going to do, so you can identify if you are on track and how well you are doing. During times of transition this certainty is not always available. It is important to be able to value the uncertainty as an important ingredient in transformation.

Another skill, which is often underdeveloped in our culture, is the ability to let go and simply flow with an experience rather than getting busy. In connecting time, you may feel disengaged from yourself and those around you. You may wish to sleep and rest. You may experience a surprising and ongoing level of fatigue. Almost an ennui, despite the interesting possibilities that you can engage in with your new-found freedom. I encourage you to have the courage to put aside your busyness and your usual way of being in the world and simply go with the experience. It is a little like being caught in a rip in the ocean. If you have skills and experience you may be able to swim out of it. But if you try and fight it you will become exhausted. Rather, let the rip carry you where it will until it lets you go. You might want to re-read about the void in *Chapter 4: Retirement fear.*

Being able to find and accept emotional support is a critical transition skill. This might mean that you have to reach out to others, to take a chance on being vulnerable and honest. It might mean that you allow yourself to access professional input and find support to negotiate this phase and to maximise your learnings.

An important transition skill is setting manageable, relevant, and achievable goals. Such a goal might simply be undertaking daily exercise or speaking to one friend every day, either in person or by phone. Loss of work often means the loss of goal setting, and therefore, loss of the satisfaction of goal kicking. The work day provides structure and is full of achievable goals – even if it is just getting to the end of the day and rewarding yourself with a well-deserved beverage. I would strongly encourage you to trial imposing a structure on your day if you feel lost or you are not being productive in some way. Setting goals is not directed towards avoiding voids. Their purpose is for you to create a life of meaning and purpose. Productivity is a key factor in successful ageing. Research has shown that 'the more productive a person is, the more protection against functional decline and death he/she enjoys'.[ii] Establish the routine of planning the day. Write up your plan the night before. Ensure that you put in the time which you will get up, and the time you will spend on activities, for example, responding to emails from 9.30 am until 10 am. Make sure you put in time for exercise! Schedule your meal breaks and your time off. It is important to plan for pleasure. For example, you might include in your plan that you will stop at 5 pm for a glass of wine while you read the paper. Include three goals that you hope to achieve. Many people have a 'To Do' list. The list is often long and unachievable. From your long list, choose a maximum of three things that you hope to achieve the next day. If you end up being able to do more, then that will be a bonus.

Note that it is important to dress well for the day. The night before, while you are planning for the next day, make a decision about what time you will be dressed and public-ready.

As we have discussed, change and transition are difficult. It is very useful to know what your tendencies are when you are dealing with a stressful situation. Do you drink more? Eat more? Smoke more? Sleep more? Maladaptive coping styles are usually about too much, or not enough.

TASK: Identifying your transition skills

1. Identify three major transitions that you have experienced in your life.

My major transitions:

a. ....

....

....

b. ....

....

....

....

c. ....

....

....

....

2. *Consider the following list of **unhelpful behaviours**. Circle any that you might have used during previous transitions. Add any that you don't see on the list.*

Not having a structure for the day	*Being stopped by fear of failure*
Not starting up conversations with other people	*Being too hard on myself and expecting too much*
Not accepting invitations	*Being angry*
Staying home	*Not communicating*
Sleeping too long or not sleeping	*Not accepting help*
Eating too much	*Not having a purpose*
Watching too much TV or other screens	*Drinking too much*
Overuse of time-wasting internet sites	*Being fearful of new learning*
Add your own:	*Add your own:*
....	....
....	....
Add your own:	*Add your own:*
....	....
....	....

3. *Consider the following list of **helpful behaviours**. Circle any that you might have used during previous transitions. Add any that you don't see on the list.*

Making social connections	*Being interested in learning*
Having fun	*Joining a group*
Keeping interested and curious	*Setting goals and being productive*
Organising time	*Scheduling a time to relax*
Exercising	*Being gentle with, and accepting of, myself*
Keeping the basics up to standard, like eating well	*Doing something enjoyable daily*
Listening to or playing music	*Being grateful*
Reading	*Giving to others*
Meditating	*Noticing what is around me by being mindful*
Accepting support	*Going with the flow*
Accepting uncertainty	*Staying well groomed*
Add your own:	*Add your own:*
....	....
....	....
Add your own:	*Add your own:*
....	....
....	....

REFLECTION

Consider developing an inventory, spreadsheet or check list of options and ideas that have worked for you, or might work for you, in managing change and transition.

If you have yet to retire, or even if you have been retired for some time, transition may still be ahead of you. However, now you have a structure for understanding your retirement process and you have identified what will help you, and what will be unhelpful, as you move through that process. The coming chapter will assist you further to journey with confidence into and through retirement, by exploring what you want to do with your life and what is important to you.

---

[i] Campbell, J. in Brown, B. (2017). *Braving the Wilderness.* London: Penguin Random House UK.

[ii] Lum, T.Y., and Lightfoot, E. (2005). 'The effects of volunteering on the physical and mental health of older people.' *Research on Aging.* 27, 31-55. doi: 10.1177/0164027504271349

Chapter 8.

Finding direction: Getting your time, energy, and interests in sync

In this chapter you are going to identify how you REALLY want to spend your time in retirement and whether you are, or will be, investing your time and energy to sync with your interests. Many people focusing on retirement can talk in depth about their investment portfolio, but it is just as important to have a portfolio of interests.

I met Therese when I was asked to work with a small group in a manufacturing plant that had been subject to a major restructure. Therese's job was safe, but she would have to accept a small promotion and as a result she would be asked to take on extra responsibilities. She was a middle manager and had been for most of her career. She did not want to progress further because she believed that she was already doing more work than she was paid for. She said, 'If I go up the ladder, I will be at work longer and doing even less of the things I really want to be doing, like travelling and spending time with my kids'.

I met Therese again, over ten years later, when she came to see me. She had retired six months previously. She was depressed and angry. She felt that she had spent her life at work, missing out on doing what she really wanted to do. Now she was retired and ready to indulge in the things she had dreamed of doing – travelling and spending time with her children –

she felt her dreams were not to be realised. She had developed a serious heart condition and plane travel was not something she was confident to undertake, nor could she obtain medical approval or travel insurance. And sadly, both of her children, along with her four grandchildren, lived overseas.

Often, we spend a lot of time doing things that are not really of interest to us. You may have a vision that this will change when you retire, but frequently it does not change — unless you take charge of it. This chapter is about ensuring that, in your retirement, you spend your time and energy doing the things that will lead you towards life satisfaction, a concept we will explore in more detail in *Chapter 18: Happiness, life satisfaction, and wellbeing.*

In this chapter you will need to move slowly. It is a chapter with a lot of work in it, rich with learning possibilities. Make no assumptions about what you will find. There are no shortcuts if you are to get the maximum benefits. Take your time and create opportunities for conversation about your thoughts and learnings. You can do the activities alone, but if you are in a relationship then I recommend that you do the work together. Alternatively, perhaps you can work with a friend or a small group. Often working with others will deepen the experience.

I will outline the task for this chapter and then describe Greg's experience in completing it. In this task you will be identifying activities, interests, themes, experiences, and states of being, according to the following three groups:

- Areas of interest: what is of interest to you now and what may interest you in the future.

- Areas of involvement: what is currently taking your time and/or energy and what is likely to take your time and/or energy in the future.

- Areas which overlap: getting your interests, time, and energy in sync, now and in the future.

At the end of the chapter I have provided you with a list of words to stimulate your thinking. Please use this word list to help you to complete the task. The list is not complete. Ensure that you add your own words and ideas. The words are largely sourced from an excellent resource called *Views from the Verandah.*[i]

TASK: Developing a portfolio of interests that will work for you now and in the future.

You may wish to complete the task twice: once for the present and once for the future.

Step 1. Areas of interest:
Ask yourself, 'What are the activities, possibilities, and topics that are of interest to me NOW?' Write a list of all the things that interest you and make you feel alive.

Step 2. Areas of involvement:
The next part of the task is to list the things that are taking up your time and/or energy NOW. These may be negative ones that suck out your time and energy; or positive ones that use your time and energy, but in return make you feel alive and re-freshed.

Step 3. Areas which overlap:
Look at your writings from Steps 1 and 2. Consider what is both of interest to you AND taking up your time or energy.

Upon completion of this task, you will have identified the areas that REALLY represent your core interests and the ones that are stealing your time and /or energy.
Consider completing this exercise again but with a FUTURE orientation to decide what might be of interest to you in the future, what might take of your time in the future, and what will be worthy of your interest, time, and energy.

REFLECTION

Ask yourself:
• Am I using my time and energy in a way that supports my areas of interest?
• Do I need to adjust how I am using my time and energy, and if I do, what will I do differently?
• Do my current interests match my expected future interests?
• How will my life look in five years if I don't make changes now?

It may be useful for you to read about Greg's experience in completing the above task. Greg was 66 and single. He came to see me because he was feeling down and irritable more days than not. Greg was good fun despite his low mood. He had been a wild lad until his mid-30s. He then realised that unless he applied himself to making some money, he might end up without a means of supporting himself. He started a small business which took ongoing time and commitment. He continued to run it, successfully surviving the ups and downs of the economy, for 31 years. Now, here he was, wondering if it had all been worthwhile.

Greg did the task for the present, firstly by completing Step 1, listing all that was currently of interest to him and would make him feel alive. Then he completed Step 2 to identify where he was putting his time and energy. This second step produced only three words. They were fitness, wealth, and security. The final step of comparing the results of Step 1 and Step 2, to identify what was both of interest to him and also taking his time and/or energy, produced no common area. When he contemplated his lists, Greg was shocked to realise that he was not doing anything on his list of things that were of real interest to him. Greg realised that he was still channelling his energy into money-making in a bid to attain the sense of security he craved 30 years ago. And he recognised that investing time into fitness was a way of dealing with his loneliness.

Greg continued to do the exercise for the future. For what will consume his time and energy in the future, Greg reconsidered his current time takers (fitness, wealth, and security). Then he looked at me and said in surprise, 'That's not what I want to be spending my time on any more'. His list of his future interests included adventure, art, community participation, security, creativity, and love-interest. He said, 'This is what I will be spending my time on and they are also my interests'. The next time I saw Greg, he said, 'I have been to see my accountant. I have decided to let go of my prioritising of security. I have put more than 30 years into focusing on security. It is holding me back. I want love and adventure, not money in the bank for my old age'.

Greg didn't change his way of life overnight, but he was a new man in my eyes. Or perhaps the scallywag he had always been was able to re-emerge. Later that year I read about him in the local paper. He was on a long-distance motor bike ride to raise money for a charity and I was glad to see that he had a good-looking companion along for the ride. Now it is your turn. Go back to the task and see what you discover.

The words

Achievement	Contemplation	Grandchildren	Nature	Solitude
Adventure	Courage	Groups	Politics	Spirituality
Animals	Creativity	Health	Power	Sport
Anticipation	Currency	Helping others	Public speaking	Study
Art	Endurance	Hobbies	Purpose	Success
Award	Employment	House	Reading	Teaching
Balance	Environment	Independence	Recognition	Travel
Car	Excitement	Leadership	Recovery	Using my skills
Caring	Family	Learning	Recreation	Volunteering
Challenge	Farming	Lifestyle	Relationships	Wealth
Changing society	Fitness	Love-interest	Relaxation	Writing
Children	Friendships	Meaning	Relevance	
Comfort	Fulfillment	Money	Security	
Community participation	Fun	Management	Sharing wisdom	
Connection	Good food	Music	Small business	

----

[i] St Luke's Innovative Resources. (2013). *Views from the Verandah*. Used with permission. Retrieved from http://innova-tiveresources.org/resources/card-sets/views-from-the-verandah-new-edition/.

Chapter 9.

Mirror, mirror, on the wall: Looking at who you are and who you will be

Who are you without your work? Sigmund Freud is credited with saying, 'Work and love … love and work, that is all there is'. He used the word 'love' to refer to meaningful relationships with significant others, while the word 'work' referred to being productively engaged. As a retired person how do you, or how will you, respond when someone asks you, 'What do you do?' This question applies equally to people who have spent their lives in unpaid roles. Work might be hard, it might be onerous, it might even be boring, but it can give us purpose, structure, connection to others, empowerment, a sense of belonging, self-efficacy, self-esteem, and identity; all things we need to feel good about ourselves.

In the last chapter you created a portfolio of interests. It is important to check that your sense of self and the way you plan to use retirement are interlocked to form a strong foundation to support your portfolio of interests. This chapter on identity will help you to grow your wellbeing and to stay on the road to life satisfaction.

A lot has been written on loss of identity in retirement. But firstly, it is important to understand what identity is, and how to create it. There are different forms and sources of identity: personal identity, group identity, and cultural identity, for example. We are limiting our discussion to personal identity. To put it simply, personal identity is a mix of all the beliefs you hold about yourself. This set of beliefs is a determinant of how you present yourself to the world and how you relate with the world. Personal identity is embedded in both our cultural and our family identities. It also comes from the groups and communities we belong to, our beliefs, our appearance, our roles, our personality, and our own experiences. At different times in our lives we can have different identities based on what we are currently prioritising. For example, sexual identity is of variable importance at different life stages. Our identity can be seen as having distinct parts that coalesce to form an ongoing whole. This 'whole' morphs and changes, but there is continuity.

Once you cease work you may feel that your identity has been seriously impacted, especially if work has been central to your identity for many years. If you have not developed other sources of identity that you value, you may have slipped into role engulfment. Role engulfment occurs when a person becomes overly identified with a persona; for example, one played out through work. In such a situation of engulfment you may feel, even when you no longer have a work role, that people are not seeing the real you if they do not know of your occupational identity. The disruption that you may feel might not be obvious to others because, to them, your occupational identity is only one part of a whole.

The various sources of our identity include:

- work – paid
- work – unpaid
- the roles we have in the family or the group we belong to – for example, being a wife or the only male in the family, or being the clever one, or the funny one
- achievements that we value, for example being a marathon runner or winning salesperson of the year
- status – such as level of education or financial wealth
- nationality
- ethnicity
- religion and belief systems

- major life events – for example, being a survivor of abuse or cancer
- social class
- friendships – who you are as a friend and who you have as friends
- sexuality
- gender
- generation – are you an X or a Y or a baby boomer or a Jones (you might need to research generation Jones if you do not know of it, especially if you were born between the mid-50s to mid-60s)
- health/fitness – loss of physical capacity is an important factor, particularly for many men
- physical characteristics – how you look (for example, thin, fat, short, bald)
- intellectual characteristics – special abilities or lack of ability
- emotional/psychological characteristics – mental health disorder, anger, resilience
- personality characteristics – easy going, fun, intense.

Our values are another very important part of our identity. Because they are so important and because they play a crucial role in retirement satisfaction, I am going to commit a chapter solely to values. For now, be aware that we bring to our identity all the information and formative experiences we have had over the course of our lives. Many of our experiences we have subconsciously discarded, and many we have retained. The retained experience drives us in our lives and the discarded has either been left behind – or is dragged along in an old sack behind us. The stories below highlight why identity can be an issue and how it can impact on our choices and our lives.

Erica had a mother who was ambitious for her children. At school Erica could never achieve to her mother's expectations. She told me, 'My mum's need for us to achieve made our lives hell. When I turned 40, I decided that I did not have to be best or top in everything or to be a career high-flyer in order to be happy. But it took me years to make this decision into something I really believed. I would find myself working into the night to make sure that I did really well in a presentation. I would feel like a failure unless I was clearly better than everyone else at whatever I was doing. So, I felt like a failure a lot! I would have called myself ambitious until I was 40. Then I realised that it is my mother who is ambitious … not me. What a relief it has been to know who I am'.

Another day I worked with a red-headed, freckled, pale-skinned male. One of the first things he said to me was, 'I am Aboriginal'. My surprised response was, 'Really?' This was not a good response, as you might imagine. He identified strongly with his Aboriginal culture. He wanted to maintain this identity and was struggling to do so because others did not identify him as being Aboriginal. His racial identity drove his political orientation, his social life, and his partner choices. It impacted on his career choice.

One woman told me, 'I don't work because in our family the women have always been full-time mothers, but I do volunteer work at the kids' school. The school asked me for help with the literacy program, but I told them I would only work in the science lab because I am a biologist'.

Paul was the oldest child in a family that struggled financially. His father was away a great deal as he worked two jobs. Paul appointed himself second father in the family. He became highly responsible, careful with money, and concerned for the safety of others he considered to be in his care. When he married, his wife complained that he was controlling. Paul had over-identified with these aspects of his role within his family of origin and was struggling to relinquish them. In Paul's mind, a good husband and father did these things and they were a strong part of his identity.

I met George and Ian quite recently when I went to dinner at a friend's house. The only person I knew was the host, but the conversation around the table interested me greatly. Two guests, George and Ian, were both retired. Both had worked at the same large university in the Faculty of Engineering. Now both had (very) part-time jobs teaching at a small adult education facility. Both answered the question, 'What do you do?' by talking about their part-time work. Both still retained their primary identity through their work.

George was happy in his response to a question about his work. He replied that he is a lecturer. But Ian, who does the same work, shrugged and said he was doing a bit of teaching. I deduced the reason for their different attitudes. In their previous positions at the university their roles included both a teaching and research component. George identified himself with the teaching part of the role and Ian identified with the researching part of the role. As a result, Ian did not feel that identifying himself to others as a teacher represented him.

Gina had worked at home raising four children. After the children left home, she spent 20 years working voluntarily as a board member with a couple of community organisations. She resigned her positions when her surgeon husband decided to retire, and they wanted to travel. Gina did not struggle with her identity because, despite losing her roles as a mother and a board member, she felt her primary identity was as a wife.

Bev's story was similar to that of Gina's. She had also stayed at home to raise four children and to support her busy professional husband. But Bev told me in some detail that her positions within a variety of community organisations were unrelated to her husband's position in the community. Bev's identity was based on being independent and a contributor. Unlike Gina, she struggled with loss of identity once she retired to be with her husband. I will tell you more about Bev in a later chapter.

Tom Fryers wrote of personal identity in his 2006 article *Work, Identity and Health.*[i] He said that 'without a clear sense of personal identity we are vulnerable to psychological injury, at risk of anxiety and depression, and social disengagement'.

Do you think that your identity is permanent, or does it change? What about your personality, is it fixed, or does it change? Most of us have had the experience of being different around different people. We know that there are times when we are outgoing and fun, and at other times we feel shy and cannot think how to be part of the group. Personality factors are not the determiners of who we are and how we are, unless they remain unchallenged. Identity is something we can mould and shape as we grow. Our beliefs and attitudes change over time. Often our sexual, political or religious affiliations, which feed into our identity, are no longer the same as they were 30 years ago. Our growth involves discarding old beliefs and patterns and re-evaluating and re-prioritising others.

Personal identity evolves over time. Problems come about when we over-identify with one or a few aspects of our identity. At a group level, over-identifying racially can lead to hostility between different racial groups. On an individual level, over-identifying with an aspect of yourself makes for problems in letting go of that aspect. People who over-identify with their psychological issue have problems letting go of it. I have had more than one long-term sufferer of depression say to me, 'But who would I be without depression?' These people feel that without their ailment they would be unsure of who they might be and how they would be in the world. The question for you is, who will I be, or who am I, without work?

Our identity is constantly evolving as we change and grow, and as the sources of our identity change. Identity is not something that you achieve once and for all. When your identity receives a major shakeup, as it does with retirement, it can usefully lead to a reassessment of identity and, if required, a decision to reinvent it. When you reflected on your findings in the task, perhaps you identified areas for reinvention and change. In the next chapter, we will look at the realities of change and how to make it happen.

TASK: Assessing your current sources of identity

The following 'sources of identity' list is not exhaustive. Add to it any other sources that are relevant to you. For example, another source is disability identity. To complete this task, simply circle the top five sources of your current identity.

IDENTITY SOURCE

Work – paid	*Major life events*
Work – unpaid	*Social class*
Roles in family or group	*Friendships*
Achievements	*Sexuality*
Status	*Gender*
Nationality	*Generation*
Ethnicity	*Health/fitness*
Religion and belief systems	*Physical characteristics*
Intellectual characteristics	*Personality characteristics*
Emotional/psychological characteristics	

REFLECTION

Consider the top five sources of your identity.
- *Are these sustainable as you age?*
- *If you are yet to retire, will these sources still be available to you once you leave the workforce?*
- *Do you need to develop other sources or reprioritise existing sources?*
- *Do you have an old identity that no longer fits?*
- *Do you want, or need, to change?*

---

[i] Fryers, T. (2006). Work, identity and health. *Clinical practice and epidemiology in mental health.* doi: 10.1186/1745-0179-2-12.

Chapter 10.

Kicking goals and managing change: Making it happen

In this chapter we are exploring goals and change. The process I will describe may be used to achieve goals and create change in any area of your life. The very purpose of this book is to enable you to clarify your retirement goals and to assist you with change – the changes you are about to encounter, or are already encountering, as you move into and experience retirement. From your reading of the previous chapters you may already have a list of changes you wish to make. Keep that list in mind as you read and learn strategies for change.

It is necessary to create goals in order to bring about the changes you want to make. Many goals are large and overwhelming. It can seem as though they are unachievable or that achieving them will take too long. Consider wanting to lose weight and how successful the average person is in achieving such a goal. It is vital to break goals into manageable chunks. Think about having to do four, or even more, years of study to get a degree. Why can so many people do this? It is because the course, aptly named, is mapped out. It is broken into chunks. One semester after another is achieved and one semester at a time is achievable. The goal of passing each subject in each semester is specific, measurable, attainable, relevant, and timely. These are the characteristics of S.M.A.R.T. goals.

S.M.A.R.T. goals increase the likelihood of success. S.M.A.R.T. stands for Specific, Measurable, Attainable, Relevant, and Timely. *Specific* requires you to set a goal with specific parameters such as where, when, and with whom. This might be similar to the course descriptions for each subject in a field of study. *Measurable* means that you have a set of criteria you use to periodically measure your progress, as in a mid-semester exam. The criteria may include what you will see, hear, and notice, or how often something will occur. *Attainable* means that it is realistic. There is no point aiming to be a volunteer in a remote mountainous region if you have a heart condition and impaired mobility. *Relevant* refers to why you are setting this goal. What will it do for you? *Timely* means you need to decide when you are going to start on this goal and when you expect to achieve it. What is your timeline for change and when will you review your progress?

I mentioned Bev in the previous chapter. She was the woman who was struggling with loss of identity on retiring. She had not engaged in paid work: rather, she had worked raising children and in community organisations. Bev developed depression when her nest emptied and she could no longer maintain her position in service organisations. She believed that her depression was due to the loss of her children and her voluntary work – that is, the loss of her mother/contributor identities which she had been heavily invested in for many years. Bev worked very hard on understanding her identity and deciding what she wished to retain and what she wished to change. She decided to reprioritise her identity sources. Bev had been a long-distance runner before babies and middle age took their respective tolls. She decided to return to her previous identity as a runner (although with age-appropriate modifications). In keeping with developing a new identity Bev made a S.M.A.R.T. goal. She wrote:

My goal is to become a runner.

- Specific: I will be able to jog one kilometre in one month's time.
- Measurable: I will review my progress every seven days by measuring the distance that I can jog.
- Attainable: Yes, confidence level 80%.
- Relevant: This goal will make me get outside and exercise which will be good for my depression and I will start to have the body I want and deserve.

- Timely: I will start today with a two-kilometre walk. I will review my progress in seven days from now and then reset my program so that I will be able to jog one kilometre in one month's time.

TASK: Making the change.

If you need to make a change, practise making that change into a S.M.A.R.T. goal. You may wish to use your work from the previous chapter where you reflected on your current sources on identity and considered whether you needed to reprioritise or develop new priorities. Ask yourself again, are your current sources of identity appropriate, sustainable and representative of you, as you are now and as you want to be in the future? If not, set a new goal.

My goal is: (name your goal)

....

....

Explain how it meets each of the following criteria:

- *Specific: ....*

- *Measurable: ....*

- *Attainable: ....*

- *Relevant: ....*

- *Timely: ....*

REFLECTION

You have written a goal and a process for achieving it.

- *Out of ten, how committed are you to following through?*
- *What would you need to increase your commitment by one or two points?*

If you have a goal that is confronting and difficult, I would encourage you to see a psychologist or to do some reading in the area. Otherwise, keep S.M.A.R.T. strategies in mind for creating change in any area of your life.

Chapter 11.

Signposts along the way: Navigating by your values

In the previous chapters we talked about identity and goals. Now we are adding in another key ingredient: values. Values, identity, and goals are interconnected. They form a personal ecology. Like all healthy ecologies, the parts must work together to support and sustain each other. There is a difference between values and goals, and it is important to be clear about this difference. Goals are something that you can achieve. You can tick a goal off your 'To Do' list. You can say that you have met, or not met, a goal. Values cannot be ticked off your To Do list. They are not something you do. They are something that you live, even if you are not aware of them or of living by them. Goals change in response to external factors such as a change in situation. Values are more enduring than goals, but they can change in priority as you grow and develop. Goals are always in the future and values are always present. Goals are personal and unique to the individual. Values are more global. Goals need to be underpinned by our values. Unless our goals and values are aligned, we will find achieving our goals a hollow victory.

Melody felt strongly about volunteering once she retired. Melody said that she felt she had a need to care and contribute as member of society. In particular, she cared about refugee welfare and environmental issues. She wanted to volunteer with an organisation working with refugees and she knew of a small group caring for the environment. Can you identify which are Melody's goals and which are her values? Her goals are volunteering in the areas she named. Her values, which are driving those goals, are caring and contribution.

Sometimes two or more values will be competing with each other when we are faced with a decision. You may be asked by your daughter to babysit on the same night that you had arranged to meet with others to prepare for a community art show. One of your values may be to be a supportive parent, and another may be to be dependable. Which value do you express?

When we are lost or unsure, our values are the neon signposts standing out in the fog telling us which way to travel. Many times, I have been confronted with a person in distress, asking, 'Tell me what to do?' Frequently my best answer is to suggest that the person stops thinking about goals and actions (doing) and thinks instead about values (being). I might respond by saying, 'Rather than thinking about what you will do, consider and decide who you will be in the situation that you are facing'.

In this chapter you will be exploring your values, and how they will inform you as you negotiate your way through the next phase of your life. Self-exploration can be hard work, but as St. Augustine, who was born in 354, wrote:

> *Men go abroad to wonder at the height of mountains, at the huge waves of the sea, at the long courses of the rivers, at the vast compass of the ocean, at the circular motion of the stars, and they pass by themselves without wondering.*[i]

It is vital that you are clear about your values when you consider who you want to be, how you want to live your life, and how you are going to achieve this vision.

Now it is time for you to consider your values. As you complete the following task, make sure that you try to separate yourself from the stories you have been told about yourself by people who have been influential in your life. Those stories and values belong to those people – for example, your mother, father, wife or husband. A friend told me over a glass of Friday afternoon wine that her mother taught her conformity by insisting that she be respectful of other people's rules. My friend willingly complied. It was not until she was in her late 20s and going off dutifully every day to work and bringing work home in the evening in order to complete it for her boss, that she discovered that her mother had been a complete nonconformist. My friend felt angry and betrayed by this new knowledge. She left her job and bought a one-way ticket overseas. And her mother's response to this independent and adventurous behaviour? She said, 'Jan I am glad to see you are finally learning to live'.

To help you to identify your own values I have included a section from Russ Harris's book The Confidence Gap.[ii] Dr Harris is a medical practitioner and psychotherapist. The list of values I have reproduced below is from a worksheet titled A Quick Look at your Values.[iii] You will find many other valuable resources on Russ Harris's websites.[iv]

Russ's method of clarifying values is different to mine, but it is well worth looking at if you wish to explore further. His list of values is:

1. Acceptance: to be open to and accepting of myself, others, life etc.
2. Adventure: to be adventurous; to actively seek, create, or explore novel or stimulating experiences
3. Assertiveness: to respectfully stand up for my rights and request what I want
4. Authenticity: to be authentic, genuine, real; to be true to myself
5. Beauty: to appreciate, create, nurture or cultivate beauty in myself, others, the environment etc.
6. Caring: to be caring towards myself, others, the environment etc.
7. Challenge: to keep challenging myself to grow, learn, improve
8. Compassion: to act with kindness towards those who are suffering
9. Connection: to engage fully in whatever I am doing, and be fully present with others
10. Contribution: to contribute, help, assist, or make a positive difference to myself or others
11. Conformity: to be respectful and obedient of rules and obligations

12. Cooperation: to be cooperative and collaborative with others
13. Courage: to be courageous or brave; to persist in the face of fear, threat, or difficulty
14. Creativity: to be creative or innovative
15. Curiosity: to be curious, open-minded and interested; to explore and discover
16. Encouragement: to encourage and reward behaviour that I value in myself or others
17. Equality: to treat others as equal to myself, and vice versa
18. Excitement: to seek, create and engage in activities that are exciting, stimulating or thrilling
19. Fairness: to be fair to myself or others
20. Fitness: to maintain or improve my fitness; to look after my physical and mental health and wellbeing
21. Flexibility: to adjust and adapt readily to changing circumstances
22. Freedom: to live freely; to choose how I live and behave, or help others do likewise
23. Friendliness: to be friendly, companionable, or agreeable towards others
24. Forgiveness: to be forgiving towards myself or others
25. Fun: to be fun-loving; to seek, create, and engage in fun-filled activities
26. Generosity: to be generous, sharing and giving, to myself or others
27. Gratitude: to be grateful for, and appreciative of, the positive aspects of myself, others and life
28. Honesty: to be honest, truthful, and sincere with myself and others
29. Humour: to see and appreciate the humorous side of life
30. Humility: to be humble or modest; to let my achievements speak for themselves
31. Industry: to be industrious, hard-working, dedicated
32. Independence: to be self-supportive, and choose my own way of doing things
33. Intimacy: to open up, reveal, and share myself – emotionally or physically – in my close personal relationships
34. Justice: to uphold justice and fairness

35. Kindness: to be kind, compassionate, considerate, nurturing or caring towards myself or others

36. Love: to act lovingly or affectionately towards myself or others

37. Mindfulness: to be conscious of, open to, and curious about my here-and-now experience

38. Order: to be orderly and organised

39. Open-mindedness: to think things through, see things from other's points of view, and weigh evidence fairly

40. Patience: to wait calmly for what I want

41. Persistence: to continue resolutely, despite problems or difficulties

42. Pleasure: to create and give pleasure to myself or others

43. Power: to strongly influence or wield authority over others, e.g. taking charge, leading, organising

44. Reciprocity: to build relationships in which there is a fair balance of giving and taking

45. Respect: to be respectful towards myself or others; to be polite, considerate, and show positive regard

46. Responsibility: to be responsible and accountable for my actions

47. Romance: to be romantic; to display and express love or strong affection

48. Safety: to secure, protect, or ensure safety of myself or others

49. Self-awareness: to be aware of my own thoughts, feelings and actions

50. Self-care: to look after my health and wellbeing, and get my needs met

51. Self-development: to keep growing, advancing or improving in knowledge, skills, character, or life experience.

52. Self-control: to act in accordance with my own ideals

53. Sensuality: to create, explore and enjoy experiences that stimulate the five senses

54. Sexuality: to explore or express my sexuality

55. Spirituality: to connect with things bigger than myself

56. Skilfulness: to continually practice and improve my skills, and apply myself fully when using them

57. Supportiveness: to be supportive, helpful, encouraging, and available to myself or others

58. Trust: to be trustworthy; to be loyal, faithful, sincere, and reliable

59. Insert your own unlisted value here:

60. Insert your own unlisted value here:

TASK: Clarifying your values

Sometimes it is easier to identify what you like about another person rather than what you like about yourself. Similarly, identifying what values you value in others can be a method of identifying your own values. Imagine that you are to be subject to an arranged marriage. You can choose the six to eight values that your intended partner will have. Be sparing and select carefully. You cannot select everything you want your spouse to have. Once you have decided your top picks for your lifelong companion, consider whether these might be your own top values.

REFLECTION

Lived values underpin life satisfaction and personal wellbeing. Consider how you are living your top values. How are you expressing those values in your daily life?

My lived values
VALUE: Examples of how I am living this value in daily life

1. ....

2. ....

3. ....

4. ....

5. ....

6. ....

By completing this chapter on values, and the preceding chapters on finding your direction and creating your identity, you have delved deeply in to the parts of yourself that may otherwise remain hidden. You will have made decisions about who you have been, about who you wish to be, and about where you want to invest your energy and time. By completing the work, you will have constructed a strong framework for a good retirement. If the retirement vision you created in *Chapter 2: Starting with the end* matches your values, direction, and identity, then it will be one of great satisfaction.

---

[i] Adels, J.H. (ed). (1987). *The wisdom of the Saints: An anthology*. Oxford: Oxford University Press.

[ii] Harris, R. (2011). *The Confidence Gap*. UK: Little, Brown Book Group.

[iii] Harris, R. (2018). *Complete worksheets for Russ Harris Books, 23-24*. Retrieved from https://www.actmindfully.com.au/wp-content/uploads/2018/06/2018_COMPLETE_WORKSHEETS_FOR_RUSS_HARRIS_BOOKS.pdf. Used with permission.

[iv] www.actmindfully.com.au; www.thehappinesstrap.com

Chapter 12.

Invisibility: The relevance deprivation syndrome

Do you recall the dawning of awareness that you were no longer quite as present and visible as you once had been in amongst the rest of humanity? Members of the opposite sex did not seem to notice you. Other people were included in the conversation before you. Younger people seemed to treat you kindly but without real interest. At some time, under cover of passing years, the relevance fairy threw a veil over you – a veil that made you hard to see.

For most people, it is an experience of change that is both confronting and challenging. What to do? Will you tear off the veil and insist that you are seen and heard? Will you, with grace and poise, incorporate the veil into your 'look' and quietly retire as a person of age? Will you move out of the world that values youth and find your own age group where you can sparkle once more? Or will you accept the invitation of our ageist society and use the veil to become part of the Greek Chorus ... a look-alike group with a collective voice, commenting on the action around them rather than being a part of the action?

The Australian Human Rights Commission Research Report of 2013 entitled *Fact or fiction? Stereotypes of older Australians*[i] states that many older Australians also report:

- service invisibility: being ignored because service people do not see value in spending time with an older person

- product invisibility: being overlooked by corporate Australia despite the financial capacity of older Australians

- relationship invisibility: feeling like they are a burden on friends and family because of the issues associated with ageing

- cultural invisibility: a lack of representation in popular culture leading to a feeling of being overlooked, devalued or ignored.

Invisibility can feel like a state of being for an older person in an ageist society.

Ageism

Robert Butler is considered to have coined the term ageism. He was an internationally recognised gerontologist and founding director of the American National Institute on Aging. As early as 1969, Robert Butler was aware of, and talked about, discrimination and stereotyping based on age.[ii]

Most stereotypes of ageing are negative. Even the aged participate in an apparently benign humour (jokes, cards etc.) based on those negative stereotypes. But such humour is powerfully perpetuating of stereotypes and therefore, of ageism. Of course, some stereotypes are positive. These include wisdom and patience. The problem with stereotypes is not that they are wrong, but that they are incomplete. I am not sure who said this, but how true!

Interestingly, 'older people who have physical and/or mental deficiencies tend to believe that ageist behaviour actually communicates a helping relationship between the younger person and the older individual, and that communication (though it is ageist) is comforting to them'.[iii]

Relevance and currency

Researchers Thomas and Blanchard say that 'the paradox of modern societies is that they provide the stability and affluence that enables many people to grow old, all the while denying older people a suitable role within the social order.'[iv]

Relevance and currency are two important concepts to ensure your visibility when you retire and as you age. Relevance and currency are about making sure that you are not a dinosaur. Dinosaurs are interesting only from a distance or at a museum. We tend not to ask their opinion or invite them to dinner. It is important that your retirement plans include a way of ensuring you maintain connection to others, and to the world, by being relevant and current.

I went to online sources to look for meanings of relevance and currency.

Relevance

The first definition came from Wikipedia[v] and made me smile as I read it twice (okay, three times) to make sure I understood it. This definition stated that 'relevance is the concept of one topic being connected to another topic in a way that makes it useful to consider the first topic when considering the second'.

The one from the Cambridge Dictionary[vi] was more useable for me. It defined relevance as 'the degree to which something is related or useful to what is happening or being talked about'.

Currency

The definition provided by The Free Dictionary[vii] was 'the state of being current; up-to-dateness'.

Relevance and currency are closely connected in the context in which we are discussing them. If you are not perceived as current, and up to date, then you are more likely to be perceived as not having relevance.

'Relevance deprivation syndrome' was a term first coined by former Australian foreign affairs minister Gareth Evans after his retirement. It is a bit tongue-in-cheek, but it will mean a lot to many people in retirement. Gareth Evans, after his retirement, went on to have a role with the International

Commission on Nuclear Non-proliferation and Disarmament. In an interview with Laurie Wilson at the National Press Club in 2010, Evans said, 'I could not be suffering less from relevance deprivation syndrome, because this is really one of the great issues of our time and we in Australia are right in the thick of it'.[viii]

The answer to avoiding relevance deprivation syndrome is to get involved and stay current. It takes work to stay involved and current and therefore to maintain relevance. It is useful to be clear about your motivation for doing this work and sustaining it.

One of the things that can undermine your motivation and undo your good intentions for staying current and relevant is unacknowledged grief or depression. Loss of any sort leads to a degree of grief. Loss of relevance and loss of status in life are major sources of grief for many in retirement. Remember how you looked forward to retirement? Remember how many people have said they envied you? How can you now complain about not feeling as important or as relevant? Doesn't everyone retire? So maybe you should just get on with it? How can you claim something as big as feeling grief?

The thing about grief is that you cannot choose not to have it – it has you. It may not be the overwhelming grief that we experience in response to death, but it is grief all the same. A quieter grief is harder to spot. Grief comes along with sadness and sometimes depressive symptoms. Depression, in addition to a down or flat mood, has as its symptoms disturbed sleep, changes to appetite, lack of motivation, irritability and loss of desire to be with others, tearfulness, difficulty concentrating and sustaining interest, difficulty making decisions, and reduced memory function. Go to *Chapter 17: The happiness hijackers*, for more information on depression, and to *Chapter 16: A bend in the road is not the end of the road*, for more information on grief.

Getting current/staying relevant

To be of relevance to others you need to be current in some way. After retirement you can achieve currency through continuing with part-time or casual work, volunteering, formal or informal study, staying up to date on current affairs, and through maintaining a passion or expertise in some area. You can maintain relevancy in the same way, but also by being a part of the lives of others. If you form good relationships with others across different generations then you will have relevance in the lives of those people and, in return, you will maintain your currency.

There is a balance to be maintained here. Why is it that you wish to sustain relevancy? Are you trying to impress younger people, of the opposite sex perhaps, with your hip ways? Are you trying to keep yourself interesting to others of your own generation? Or, are you trying to ensure that you can move across different age groups?

Really have a think about this. I have worked with people who believe that they have their own generation covered. They want to be able to move intergenerationally. It is important to be able to move between different age groups, but have a long, honest think. The reality for some is that they value the younger generations more than people of their own age. I am not passing judgement on this. Just be clear about what you want and why.

Your goal will direct your actions. There are basic skills to use whether you want to maintain relevancy for improving your relationships with one generation or all generations. I have noticed, in working with some retired people, that they have an attitude that they have done the hard work, and they no longer have to try. It is a position of, 'take me as I am'. There is worth in this position, but not if it comes with an interpersonal laziness. It also tends to come across as pompous, a type of been-there-and-done-that.

Do you recall Greg, my 66-year-old retired and reborn scallywag from *Chapter 8: Finding direction*? Before we did the work on finding his direction, he would make me laugh with stories of past exploits. However, I noticed that all his stories were of the past. I asked him to complete time circles (as in the following task). When he did so, he identified that his interests were in the past and that he closed down thoughts about the present and future because of his fears around both. This impacted on his sense of currency and therefore his relevance. He decided that he wanted to improve his currency and relevance by being less in the past and more in the present and future. Complete the following circle task for yourself and see what you discover.

TASK: Identifying your orientation to the past, present and future

AS YOU ARE NOW

Divide this circle into three parts, representing the amount of time you spend thinking or talking about the past, the amount of time you spend thinking or talking about the present, and the amount of time you spend thinking or talking about the future. You might want to draw an extra circle or two for different behaviours in different situations and with different people.

AS YOU WISH TO BE

As before, divide this circle into three parts. But this time divide the circle as it needs to be divided in order to maintain your currency in the world. Divide it to represent the amount of time you believe you should spend thinking or talking about the past, the amount of time you should spend thinking or talking about the present, and finally the amount of time you should spend thinking or talking about the future. If you drew extra circles for AS YOU ARE NOW, then re-draw those here and complete them.

There is no right or wrong answer in this exercise. But generally, a healthy response will be weighted towards larger present and future segments. This is an interesting exercise to do with a partner.

REFLECTION

It is important to respect the past and let it inform us. But it is only a backdrop. It is critical to be able to be fully present in the present. It is essential to have plans for the future. Try to work towards a balance that will help to keep both you and your life current and relevant.

> Examine your own results. What do you need to do?
> - *Are you too much in the past? If so, what can you do to move into the present?*
> - *Are you too much in the present, and if so, what can you do to acknowledge the past and ensure the future?*
> - *If you are too much in the future, are you just avoiding the present? What can you do to embrace the here and now?*

Tom is a Vietnam veteran. He drew his two circles. Between his AS YOU ARE NOW circle and his AS YOU WISH TO BE circle there was a big difference in how much time he spent talking about the past and the future. He realised he was constantly thinking about the past in his AS YOU ARE NOW circle. In his AS YOU WISH TO BE circle, Tom decided that he wanted to reduce this past focus and to spend more time thinking about the present and a future that he was having difficulty imagining. Looking at his results, Tom decided to get the counselling his wife had been asking him to have for many years.

Rob found that he had little to say about the present, but he said a lot about the past and future. After completing the AS YOU ARE NOW circle, with its large past and future and its small slice of present, he looked at me wryly and said, 'No wonder people seem to find me boring. I am not actually do-ing anything. I am all talk'. He proceeded to draw an AS YOU WISH TO BE circle that increased his present to one third of the circle as a start point. Then he said to me, 'So, help me fill in this slice!'

Ideas for staying current and maintaining relevance

If you find that you are heavy on the past, re-look at the task you completed in the chapter on identity (*Chapter 9: Mirror, mirror, on the wall*). Perhaps your sources of identity are no longer current. Try to develop your interest in the present and future. Re-look at the results of the work you did in *Chapter 8: Finding direction*. Your own present might be a little empty and so might your future. If it is, try to be interested in others and use your curiosity to find out what is relevant now. Live a little through others. So long as you are non-judgemental and able to withhold on giving advice, then people will love to talk to you. It is healthier to talk to real people with real emotions and real stories than to watch TV. It also brings you connection, which is another of the critical elements of both a happy, successful retirement and personal wellbeing.

Keep up with new methods of communicating. This is one of the most important ways of maintaining your currency. Get technology savvy. Communication is technology based. Learn, if you don't know how. Don't be embarrassed. Laugh about it. Include others. Make it a social event. Others love to feel they know more than you and then to impart knowledge.

Bringing back memories is dangerous territory. A quick relevancy death is to hark back to your memories from the 1970s in response to people who are dealing with the same issue, but many years later. Your experience from 50 years ago is unlikely to be immediately relevant, or even very interesting, to someone dealing with the here and now. To maintain your currency, use the opportunity to discover why, and how, the apparently same issue is now different. Be curious. Learn rather than teach. Take a seat rather than the platform. Speak to the topic if you are asked but be brief. Make your experience relevant to the listener. Leave your listener wanting more rather than less.

Also, stay away from clichés such as: 'in my day ...', 'when I was a boy ... ', 'in my time ... ', 'we used to... ', 'it was better/different in the old days', and 'things have changed'. All of these clichés indicate someone who is oriented to the past, and to themselves in the past. To be relevant you need to be a part of something in the here and now, and a part of something that is bigger than you.

Keep fit. It is one of the factors that leads to wellbeing and a mentally happy retirement. When you keep fit and toned you look better and more present. You are less likely to drag your body around. It is easy to bring to mind images of older people who look old and those who, although the same age, look young. It is not about being less wrinkled or thinner. It is about being fit, holding your body upright, having a bit of a spring in your step and a brightness of eye.

If you have aches and pains or physical problems don't make these your topic of conversation. I went to a gym class about two months ago. We were asked to partner up and an older lady immediately picked me. She spent the entire time telling me of her body woes. She really did have quite a few, but by the end that is how I saw her … as a list of ailments. I wonder if a younger person would have indulged in this behaviour even if they did have a list of problems? I do not know at what age discussing bodily functions becomes acceptable, but perhaps it should be confined to a very small and carefully selected few people. At the same class I initially had to follow an older man in the circuit. He was lean and dressed in current gym clothing. He was a bit slow and I knew I could go faster than him. As a result, I started to feel quite good about myself. At the end of the class our teacher, Natasha, said to him, 'You had a birthday last week Jim. How old are you now?' Jim quietly gave his age and I quietly gasped. He was 15 years my senior.

Like Jim, dress for the current period. I don't mean dressing as a young person, but to be seen as current it will help if you keep your clothes modern and your hair cut and styled. When you get up each morning, do you dress for the day so that you will be proud of your appearance should someone arrive, or do you go for a comfortable tracksuit look?

Another hallmark of older people is their view that the world is not as good as it was. Stay optimistic. Again, it does not matter what age you are, being a pessimist is a bit of a downer for all around you.

This chapter will help you to find a way to negotiate with the relevance fairy and escape her invisibility veil! In an ageist society this is difficult to achieve. Perhaps you can be the change you want to see in our society.

---

[i] https://www.humanrights.gov.au/sites/default/files/document/publication/Fact%20or%20Fiction_2013_WebVersion_FINAL_0.pdf.

[ii] Achenbaum, W. A. (2014). 'Robert N. Butler, MD (January 21, 1927-July 4, 2010): Visionary leader.' *The Gerontologist.* 54(1), 6-12. https://doi.org/10.1093/geront/gnt015.
[iii] Nelson, T.D. (2011). 'Ageism: The strange case of prejudice against the older you'. In R.L. Wiener & S.L. Willborn (Eds.), *Disability and Ageing Discrimination* (pp. 37-47). doi:10.1007/978-1-4419-6293-5.
[iv] Thomas, W.H., and Blanchard, J.M. (2009). 'Moving beyond place: Aging in community.' *Generations*, 33(20), 12-17.
[v] https://en.wikipedia.org/wiki/Relevance.
[vi] https://dictionary.cambridge.org/dictionary/english/relevance.
[vii] https://www.thefreedictionary.com/currency.
[viii] Evans, G. (2010). National Press Club Address, Canberra. 18 February, 2010. http://www.icnnd.org/transcripts/100218_evans_npc.html.

Chapter 13.

Relationships and retirement: Looking after each other … and your children

If there is a major shift in your life that causes you to adjust your self-perception, your identity, your self-concept, your purpose and direction, that makes you think about yourself differently, that changes how you see yourself in relation to others, that changes how you present yourself to others, that changes how you dress every day, that changes what you do every day, and that changes how much money you have, it will be no surprise that your relationships with others will change, too.

Wife, mother, grandmother, worker, home maker, relationship manager

I think that women deserve a special mention here. Much of the research supports the experience of many women that their roles are pivotal and multiple – and include managing family relationships. Of course, this does not exclude the role undertaken by many men. Yet, women report that they are working outside the home, inside the home, have adult children staying on within the home, are providing child care for grandchildren, caring for ageing parents and sometimes an ill spouse or relative, and, with increasing frequency, someone in their circle of care has a mental health disorder. The current generation of women are pioneers in managing this constellation of factors. They have not had the required skills demonstrated to them by their mothers or grandmothers. Often, they are learning from each other. Often, they are overwhelmed. From a retirement perspective, I have regularly heard a woman express the fear that if she leaves the workforce she will not have an 'out' and will be consumed by family demands. If you are in this group, it might be wise to pay special attention to this chapter and the next on relationships.

Our relationships underpin our platform of security. This platform wobbles precariously during the process of transition and change. We have to focus on adjusting our centre of balance in order not to fall. And what is happening to our relationships as we do this?

TASK: Getting your relationships into focus

Step 1. Make a list of the most important relationships in your life. These may be obvious to you but try to think broadly. They may include a relationship with an ex-partner as well as a current partner. They may include work relationships if you are still in the workforce or relationships with volunteers if you are an unpaid worker. They may include a relationship with someone who has left you through death but who still lives on in your life in some way.

....

....

....

....

....

....

....

....

....

Step 2. Draw up a chart of three vertical columns. In the first, write the list of names of the people you have chosen as comprising your most important relationships. In the next column, rate each of those relationships in terms of how important it is to you. Rate from 1 to 10 with 10 being the most important. You can assign the same number to more than one relationship but try to be brutally honest with yourself in order to benefit in this exercise. In the third column, rate how much time and/or thought you give to each relationship. Rate it from 1 to 10 with 10 indicating the highest investment of time and/or thought.

Relationship	Importance (1-10)	Investment (1-10)

REFLECTION

Study the list and consider the outcome.
- *Do you put your time and/or thought into the relationships which are of most value to you?*
- *Do you need to re-prioritise your relationships or reorganise your investment of time and emotional effort?*
- *Do you need to let go of, or change, some relationships because the ongoing investment has not paid dividends and appears unlikely to do so?*

Primary relationships

We are focusing on your primary relationships. Typically, primary relationships are those with an intimate adult, and with your children. At retirement those children are usually adults. Primary relationships have the most impact on our happiness. In this chapter we will limit our discussion to the impact of your retirement on your adult children. The following chapter will focus solely on retirement and intimate relationships.

Relationships with adult children

It is interesting to me that I have been asked for help by the adult children of parents who are moving into retirement. The adult children seem a little confused and unsure about how to help their parent/s during this life phase. Frequently, I have noted that they seem anxious about a spike in conflict between their parents and feel that their parents do not seem to be on track ... whatever track that is.

Most children want to help their parents but are unsure how to do it. Nevertheless, there are some children who seem to have a different problem. They are *too* sure that they know what their parents should be doing and do not hesitate to say so.

Retirement can be a time when existing conflicts, fractures or tensions in the parent-child relationship become more apparent. As you look for new identities, and new ways of finding meaning in your life, your children may feel sidelined. Perhaps you are no longer so accessible to provide child care. Perhaps your days are less predictable and so it is harder for your children to get hold of you when they want you. Perhaps you want to see more of them now that you have more time and it is putting pressure on them.

Increasingly, adult children need financial assistance from their parents in order to be able to purchase a house. It is not to your children's benefit if you are no longer earning. As a parent you might be asked to go guarantor. If you do enter into a financial arrangement with your child, ensure that you obtain good quality legal advice. I know of one kind dad who postponed his retirement in order to co-purchase a house with his son. The son found a partner who moved into the new house. All looked rosy until the partner left and demanded financial compensation as a de facto. The son had a car accident during the unpleasant proceedings of separation, and was unable to work for an extended period. The kind dad lost his financial position and retirement went off the radar completely.

Good communication is always the key to resolving issues such as your children's concerns and desire to help you. Perhaps ask them to read this book and then use it as a talking point. Discuss what parts of the book are relevant to you, what parts are not, and why.

Intimate relationships

The next chapter is directed towards those who have a life partner. However, it describes skills that are useful across a variety of relationships. Our primary relationships are critical to our wellbeing. Intimate relationships are of particular importance. We will explore important skills to protect relationships during retirement.

Chapter 14.

Dancing to a different tune:
Learning new steps

Retirement can challenge our relationships in surprising ways. And the outcomes can be just as surprising. Sometimes the shakeup revitalises, sometimes it tears apart, and sometimes it leads to new relationships or re-prioritising of old relationships. Many things change when you retire – how you feel about yourself and yourself in the world, and how you are perceived by others and by your partner. When you change, your partner will change in response and, inevitably, the relationship changes.

Of course, while some couples seem to sail through retirement transitions many others struggle. Have you and your partner learned to dance together or are you still stepping on each other's toes? Often, we develop a way of dancing together that may not look graceful; but we at least avoid having our toes hurt. However, if the music changes the dance will change. Sometimes toes get hurt in the process. In this chapter we will look at different relationship combinations in retirement. I will describe each of these combinations in detail. Within each I have placed a lot of useable information, plus specific skills that will relate to you regardless of which combination you are in.

In this chapter we will explore when:

- one of you retires and one does not. This looks at the skill of talking together.
- you both retire at the same time. This looks at conflict styles.

- you both move to retirement but maintain part-time work, paid or unpaid. This looks at relationship phases.

In the following chapter we will examine when:
- one of you retires from full-time work and one of you has not been in the workforce for a period of time. This looks at role specificity.
- your retirement, or that of your partner, is not voluntary or planned. This looks at the stages of grieving.

Each of the combinations brings its own challenges. There are also challenges that are common to all of them. So whichever combination fits your situation, or even if you are not in one of the described relationship combinations, do read the information in each.

When one of you retires and one does not

If you are the one retiring ... woohoo! It is going to be great. You will have all the time you have always wanted. Perhaps you plan to contribute more to the housework or maintaining the garden. You predict that you will have time to do all of these things and more. Your partner will continue to bring in money ... so eeeeasy! If you are the one staying on at work, you might feel pleased. Now you can hand over the mundane tasks of cleaning and cooking and be cared for without guilt. Or you might feel resentful – you have worked hard all your life and now you are still working. Or you may not be sure how you feel.

Jeff was pleased and relieved when Leanne retired. She disliked her job and felt taken for granted. She had become anxious about her work load and was spending a lot of nights doing work at home. Jeff dreaded coming home each night to hear her complaints. They both believed that Leanne's retirement would work well for them. But they struggled and argued when Leanne retired. For the first year, each blamed the other for the struggle. Jeff felt keenly his disappointment that

Leanne did not become cheerful and motivated. 'Why can't you EVER be satisfied?' he asked her. Leanne felt she had finished her working life on a sour note. She was sad and disappointed, but she did not feel she could talk (complain) about it to Jeff. Rather, she struggled with believing that Jeff had dropped the ball when it came to sharing the house duties. Again, she felt taken for granted. 'I don't mind if Jeff does less around the house now that I am not working, but he should at least discuss it and not just expect me to do it all', she said.

No matter what you expect, when one of you retires and one stays on at work, things change. Enter inequity. Enter new expectations. Enter role changes. And these changes are in addition to all the other transitional challenges that come with retirement.

When you are both working it is as though you are travelling in the same direction and often at approximately the same pace. When one stops it can feel as though your gears are no longer meshing. Of course, for some couples this is not the case. For some, the retired person manages to smooth the path of the worker and to enjoy doing so. In return the worker is appreciative. For others, the retired person resents the amount of time that the worker expects to be spent on smoothing (housework, shopping, cooking) and the worker resents the retired person's easy (and money-sucking) lifestyle.

Greg and Penny had a difficult time when Greg retired. Penny had been at home when the children were young. She returned to work because they needed more money to keep the children at the schools they had chosen and to pay the mortgage; a typical picture. Penny quite enjoyed her job – not the actual work, but her co-workers. She really enjoyed having more money, and money that she considered to be her own, even though her wage was responsible for maintaining the household day-to-day. Now Penny and Greg had only one young adult child at home, so Penny was doing a lot less juggling of work and house. Greg was offered a redundancy that they both agreed he should take. At first, they were both optimistic that this would work out well, not just financially but practically. And it did. Greg enjoyed the daily domestic routines and having the meal ready for Penny when she came home. Gradually it changed as the holiday feeling wore off. Penny found little pleasure in having the small house chores completed and the cooking done. She was surprised to find that she felt resentful. She was aware that she now felt a little like a visitor in her home and as such felt disengaged from her former life.

With that disengagement she started to look at Greg more critically. Greg had started well in his banking career but did not progress as expected. This was why Penny had had to return to work. Penny said, 'I had to go back to work because Greg could not earn enough. I had to leave my job of raising the children, which I loved. I worked two jobs; one outside the home and one inside. Now Greg has swanned in when all the hard work of child rearing is over, and he can enjoy himself. I have missed out at both ends. It makes me feel uncomfortable to be admitting this. It is selfish of me. Greg has always done the best he can. But I hate coming home to find him in shorts and an old T-shirt with a beer in his hand. He was much more attractive when he wore a suit and had credibility in the world'.

Listening to Penny, I could hear that she was expressing both old and new resentments. An old resentment had surfaced. She resented that Greg could not make sufficient money to enable her to stay at home to raise the children as she had wanted to do. Her new resentment was that Greg was without the work load which she had to deal with when she was at home. This new resentment is layered on top of the old one. Greg may, or may not, have been aware of the old dormant resentment. If he was not aware of it, he might have trouble dealing with it as well as dealing effectively with the new one. Penny and Greg, like many retiring couples, would have to do some hard talking. Their conversation would need to be honest and represent them authentically. Without this, the resentments between them might fester and find expression in small ways.

What I am describing are common experiences. You and your partner may not have this experience. You may have something similar, but different. Your way of resolving your differences will depend on what works in your relationship. It is not a one-size-fits-all. If, like Penny and Greg, you need to do some honest talking, then it takes preparation and courage. Don't rush into it. Make sure you reflect on what is happening for you and decide what you want or need to change.

Talking together skills

You need to know what you want to say if you want to be heard and understood. That might sound obvious, but it is not. Some people are internal thinkers and some people are external thinkers. Internal thinkers do their thinking inside their own head. External thinkers do it outside their heads, by talking.

An internaliser and externaliser combo can be good together. The talker sends a word stream past the internaliser. The latter listens and considers the message while the externaliser thinks out the problem aloud. But they can also frustrate each other. Internal thinkers often find external thinkers overwhelming. They do not understand why that person goes on and on. The externaliser thinks that the internaliser is not thinking at all, perhaps not even listening, and is making decisions without thinking it through adequately.

Similarly, other combinations have pros and cons. Two externalisers can talk through an issue until they find resolution and obtain a good insight into each other's point of view. But it can be hard for each person in a couple comprised of two externalisers to get enough air time. Two internalisers might not have much sharing or discussion and sometimes it can be hard for them to get on board together, and to feel connected.

Regardless of whether you are an internal thinker or an external thinker, you do need to know what you want to say if you want to be heard and understood. That does not mean that you have it all sorted before you talk. But it does mean that you need to know WHAT you are talking about and WHY you are talking about it.

Jan and Michael came to me to do some retirement planning. Michael was speaking about contacting their financial adviser to decide what their frequency limits might be for adventure travel. Jan responded with cool agreement. However, she continued to lead the conversation off track with small comments about Michael's lack of fitness, weight, and health. It was apparent that there was a difference between WHAT Michael was talking about, and WHY and WHAT Jan was talking about. When I noted this to them, Jan immediately reacted. She said, 'Why are we talking about how often we will be able to go to these remote places when Michael is overweight and unhealthy? I am not going to be stuck in the back of beyond while he has a heart attack'. Here Jan is making the tactical error of making claims or statements about Michael rather than speaking about herself, her concerns and needs. Michael responded with, 'You only see the worst, Jan. You worry about everything and, if I listen to you, we will go nowhere and do nothing'. Michael has made the conflictual conversation blunder of talking about Jan as though he has some special powers of observation or of knowledge.

The what and the why of conversation sets the context. Within that context you get to speak about yourself, NOT about the other person. Jan said that Michael is overweight and unhealthy. It would have been more powerful if she had spoken about herself, rather than making statements about Michael.

You may be familiar with the idea of 'I' statements. I statements are about a way of talking in difficult situations that reduces the conflict and increases the chance that you will be heard and understood. In general, the rules are that you speak only about yourself. Avoid the word 'you' and speaking for and about the other person.

First, describe the situation which you need to speak about. Avoid blaming. Speak only from your own perspective. Second, describe how you feel about it. Again, without blaming the other person. Third, suggest a solution, describing what you would prefer. Lastly, ask the other person whether that is workable for him or her.

Jan might have said, 'When we talk about going to remote places I start to worry about Michael's weight and health. I fear him having a heart attack in a place where I will be alone and unable to get help. I want to deal with this before we consider going away to remote places. Could we do that, Michael?'

There is a wealth of information on the internet about I statements. I suggest you research it, perhaps together, if you wish to learn more about talking, so that you are both successfully heard and able to manage difficult conversations. Perhaps you can do the research before you undertake the next task.

TASK: Talking together successfully

Think of a conversation you need to have with your partner. Start with something that is on the easier side of incendiary. Try using the structure below to frame your conversation.

- *When … (describe the situation from your perspective, using I rather than you)*
- *I feel/think/wonder/sense …*
- *I would prefer …*
- *How would that be for you?*

REFLECTION

How did you go? Do you need to learn more? Sometimes people find that their best attempts are thrown off course by someone responding with a red herring. Suddenly you are off track and possibly defending yourself. Avoid this by simply ignoring the response and repeating your statement.

This skill of talking together successfully is easy to understand but difficult to put into practice, especially if emotions are running hot. It is a skill that is best learned together so that you can have fun and help each other. However, if your partner is not willing you will gain a great deal by putting it in practice yourself, even if you think it is your partner who needs to improve! Conflict skills which are discussed in the next section will help you to understand your own style.

When you both retire at the same time

Pamela told me sadly, 'Paul has been a good man and a good provider. While we were both working, we rubbed along together happily enough. Now we have both retired. We planned to retire at the same time so we would both be free and able to do things together. But it is as though we no longer know each other. We used to want the same things, which was to go to work, pay the bills, and have a nice simple life together. Now we want different things. He has changed. He says it is his last chance to have a bigger life than the one we have been living. I just want to do as we have always done, but I don't know that he can live with that and be satisfied. And I don't know that I can live with him'.

I was puzzled by Pamela's description of her problems. 'Did you and Paul talk about what you both wanted before you went into retirement?' I asked. 'Of course,' said Pamela, 'but life changes, doesn't it? Our share portfolio is not worth what it was. Paul is easier-going about money than I am. The change in our financial circumstances doesn't worry him. We had planned to drive around Australia and explore it at leisure, but I don't want to end up being without money as we get older or without money to help the kids if they need it. Paul is resentful of me because he said I am not doing what we agreed to do. He is right, but things change.'

Retirement can throw even an apparently solid relationship into confusion. Pamela and Paul will have to do some honest talking. If they have been used to doing so in their relationship it will be easier for them. However, this is not easy when roles have been specified and followed for some time. When you have had stable roles, it seems that there is a stable base from which to make predictions about your partner and his or her wants and responses. But life, and people, will both change. That change can be unsettling and when we are unsettled, we often look for someone else to blame.

It will be great if Pamela and Paul can learn the skill of speaking only about themselves and not about, or for, the other, as Jan and Michael (whom you met previously) had done. In addition, it may be useful for them to consider how they have traditionally dealt with conflict in their relationship.

Relationship conflict skills

The Thomas-Kilmann Conflict Mode Instrument[i] is an easy way of looking at yourself in conflict. Another such instrument, developed by Dr Ron Kraybill over a period of some years, is the Kraybill Conflict Style Inventory.[ii] Both identify five styles, labelled differently, that people use in dealing with conflict. The styles are competing, collaborating, compromising, avoiding, and accommodating. We all use a little bit of each style in different situations and with different people. You may discover that you use a different style at home than you use at work, or with your children versus with your partner. You may find that you generally use one style, but in very important or difficult matters you go to another style.

Consider the five styles and reflect on your own behaviour. It is particularly useful to talk together with your partner about how you see your own conflict style and how you perceive that of your partner.

One style is COMPETING. This style describes those people who are out to win and can be quite pushy about it. If using this style, you are putting your own views or needs first.

A second style is COLLABORATING. Collaborators want to problem-solve together. They want to be jointly focused on the identified issue and to work through it together. They may have a preferred view, but they are able to listen and incorporate another's view point and be flexible in their approach. They achieve this through talking and listening.

Another style is COMPROMISING. Compromisers want to find a solution that satisfies both parties and they are willing to give a bit, on the expectation that the other party will give a bit too. They want to see that each person is doing their bit and giving something to resolve the conflict.

Yet another style is AVOIDING. Avoiders do just that. They withdraw from difficult situations. This withdrawal might not be obvious until you have to deal with this person regularly. Then the pattern will begin to emerge and your frustration will begin to rise. Avoiders do not deal with your issues, or their own. Avoidance can be achieved through procrastination. 'I will talk about this problem if you want to, but not right now.' It can be achieved through denial. 'It is not that bad, I don't know why you are going on about it.' Some avoiders will simply slip away when issues are raised. Others are masters of the red herring and diverting of the topic. 'Yes, sure, but that reminds me, shouldn't we give George a ring about … '

And finally, there is ACCOMMODATING. Accommodators will give in to ensure that there is as little conflict as possible. If an accommodator's opinion differs from the other person's and they sense conflict, they do not pursue their own needs and wants. They can appear to be easy-going and generous, but this tends to be another form of avoidance. All too often, the resentment goes underground and pops out unexpectedly, typically on small unrelated matters.

It is tempting to value, or to be critical of, one style more than another. However, each has its place. It is important to have the capacity to use each appropriately and flexibly. If you have a partner who continually uses avoidance you might be highly critical of this approach. But it has its place. There are situations where it needs to be employed. Yet, if it is the only strategy that someone uses then it will be very frustrating for the person on the experiencing end of it. It will be very hard to get decisions made and almost impossible to make joint decisions. Avoiders create strangers in a relationship and competitors create enemies. When you read the description of a competitor you may feel that this, too, is a style that you could rightly criticise. Even so, it also has its place. But like any style, if you use it exclusively, it will create problems.

TASK: Understanding your conflict style

 *Create a bar chart. At the base of the vertical axis put the number 0; then in regular lots of 10 mark the axis up to 100. On the horizontal axis write the five conflict styles. Think about yourself in your relationship. Mark on the chart how fre- quently you operate in each style within your relationship. You may need to create another chart if either you or your partner are very different in a particular part of your lives together. For example, John rated himself as 20 (low) on competing. But he knew that he was reactive about money. He created another chart and labelled it MONEY. He considered his style with his wife when discussing their money and investments. In this chart he rated himself as 80 on competing.*

REFLECTION

 *Consider your own conflict style. Are you satis- fied with it? Is there anything you need to change? Share your information with your part- ner. Does your partner see you the same way or differently? If your partner sees you differently ask why. Try to listen without justifying or defending yourself. Is there something you need to change or to work on together?*

When you both move to retirement but maintain part-time work

In some ways this can be an ideal arrangement. It means that you both continue to have purpose, structure, connection to the greater world, and an income stream. It can also work well if the work is voluntary or something for which you have a passion. The passion replaces the money. The downside is that you are still both tied by commitments.

Some couples will find that, if they retire at the same time but both have part-time work, they will come out of their companionate relationship (where being companions rather than lovers is primary) and the relationship will get a fresh start. It is a shot in the arm without the challenge of unstruc- tured days and no money coming in.

Tony and Mary retired at the same time from jobs which had provided an income rather than satisfaction. Tony took up a paid casual position with the local repertory group as their general hand. Mary found a casual position doing running repairs on clothing during modelling shoots. At the end of their respective work days they had stories to tell each other and a sense of achievement.

Relationship phases

I will describe the phases of intimate long-term relationships which may provide you with a way of understanding your own relationship. Relationships move through phases as they develop over time. They begin with oneness. This is the phase where you are completely involved with each other and have a wonderful sense of being as one person. Sadly, it does not last.

The second phase is about disharmony. As the sense of oneness wears off, it is often replaced by a feeling of disappointment. The things that initially attracted you will now annoy you. You loved the way she was so calm and quiet when you have always been so loud and reactive. But now she is a bit dull. Where is the fun? Why doesn't she want to go out more often? You loved the way he had so many friends and would laugh so heartily and so easily. But now you wish his friends would not come over so frequently. Why can't he just tell them not to come? Why does he have to laugh like that? He sounds ridiculous. Some couples do not move beyond this stage.

The third phase is about togetherness; accepting and valuing the other person. You value them, not for what they give to you and how they help you to feel good, but as a trusted and loved companion. It is a mature acceptance that I am me and you are you, and we can share important parts of our lives, but we do not have to be as one person, nor do you have to live the way I want you to live. In this phase of trusting companionship there may or may not be intimacy. And that is a topic for another book!

Sometimes when we move through a life transition such as retirement, our relationships can cycle through these phases once again.

TASK: Reviewing your relationship

Are you in:
1. Oneness
2. Disharmony
3. Togetherness

REFLECTION

Discuss this with your partner if he or she is willing. Might it be worth having a relationship review or check up with a relationship counsellor? This is a worthwhile and rewarding endeavour for any relationship.

I encourage all couples to have a six-month tune up. Most couples turn up in my office when the relationship is no longer sustainable, and they are angry and desperate. The idea of seeing a third party is not to point fingers or to blame, but to create a safe space for each couple to deal with their own challenges and to make choices about what to keep, what to do differently, and what to let go.

---

[i] http://www.kilmanndiagnostics.com/overview-thomas-kilmann-conflict-mode-instrument-tki.

[ii] Kraybill, R. (2005). *Style Matters: The Kraybill Conflict Response Inventory*. Riverhouse ePress.

Chapter 15.

More new steps:
The dance continues

In the preceding chapter we looked at combinations in retirement where both members of a couple were, or are, in the workforce. In this chapter we are looking at other combination styles. Again, even if you are not in one of these combinations I believe that you will gain from reading the information I have placed in each.

When one of you has retired from full-time work and one of you has not been in the workforce for a period of time

Alan was a tradesman who worked in a large hospital. He was one of the longest serving workers in the maintenance department, so he had a reputation for being the go-to man. He was the union representative. He ran the social club and organised all the events. He had a wife of 40 years with whom he had a 'good marriage'. Life was very pleasant for Alan and he expected it to get even better when he retired. But once he retired, he was disappointed. He told me about his wife, 'She is a good woman and runs a shipshape home. So why am I so angry with her? She hasn't done anything wrong, not really. But she seems to have changed. We just don't get on any more'.

Suddenly it can seem like the other person is someone you no longer know or with whom you no longer fit. I do not know what happened to Alan as our conversation took place in passing while I was doing a hospital visit. He was heading back to visit his old department 'just to catch up on the gossip'. While I listened to him, I wondered if he and his wife had run into role specificity problems.

Role specificity

Role specificity is an important factor in retirement relationships. Some couples have very clear roles within their relationship. Sometimes these roles have been discussed and agreed on and sometimes they have just grown organically as life unfolded.

I play tennis with Ang and Ron. They were talking about themselves and their adult children as we stopped to pick up balls. As many words as balls go over the net when I play tennis. Ang stayed at home when their three children were small. About 20 years ago, Ang wondered if she might try to get back into the workforce. This was the first time that she and Ron actually talked about who was doing what in their partnership. Ron was not keen for Ang to take on work outside of the home. But Ang did return to work, and then retired early when workplace conflict began impacting on her health. She is busy and happy with the life she has created. Ron remains as the bread winner. Their son, Will, has been married for three years and has one child. Will and Jess have a very different arrangement. According to Ron and Ang, the young couple carefully negotiated who would do what within the marriage. Ang reflected that there seems to be much more sharing but there also seems to be more conflict about who is doing what and more need for discussion.

Is Ron and Ang's way better than Jess and Will's? No, I do not think so. But for many retiring couples the challenge is moving from role specificity, like that of Ron and Ang, to role sharing, as Will and Jess do. Keep this concept in mind as you read on.

David was a charming man. He was used to running his own show and had been a successful manager of a small but busy IT area. He was a lateral thinker and liked to create change and to innovate. Our work began when he retired. His wife, Sue, was a homemaker. She welcomed David's retirement ... until he had been home for three months. The fun had definitely worn out by then. David had so many good ideas about how Sue could do things differently or – yes, 'better' – around the house. He simply had too much to say about systems that had been in place and functioning well for a long time. Sue began to resent David and his intrusive 'helpful' comments. David needed to find an outlet for his innovative brain or to at least take more time and care in making and suggesting change. David very quickly caught on to this when I used an organisational framework with him. Did he recall new CEOs or managers who came in with their new broom and did a lot of sweeping? Yes, he did. Did it work well? 'Sometimes it did,' he said, 'but there was always a fall-out and good people left.' 'Hmm,' I responded, 'pity if Sue was one of the good people who left.' David quickly changed his approach.

At least Ron and Ang, who I mentioned earlier, are doing more talking and reflecting now as they watch their adult children negotiate their marriages. They are starting to talk and prepare for Ron's retirement. Ron will need to follow in David's footsteps by being respectful of Ang's turf and slow to suggest change when he retires. Ang, however, will have to share her patch.

Sharing

Ang has already spoken to me about sharing her patch. She is a little concerned. What will happen when Ron is home each and every day? What will happen to her routine? How will she have the gardening club for champagne and fun in their little house with Ron hanging around? How will she tell him to leave for the day when she knows that he is interested in gardening and has always shown interest in the club? Ang does not want to share her club. And not only that, 'It is ridiculous, I know,' says Ang, 'but I hate the way he vacuums. He doesn't do it often but when he does, he misses whole parts of the room. And when he puts on the washing, he never sorts the colours. I feel so petty saying this, but it really annoys me. Ron says, "Can't I even put on the washing properly?" And I feel like a prat, but I also want to say, "NO, YOU CAN'T!""

Ang is going to have to make space for Ron. She needs to work out what part of home life she wants to share and what part she wants for herself. Ron is going to have to take it slowly as he tries to work out where he wants to integrate into the home scene. There is no point in Ron doing what he might think is the right thing by undertaking domestic chores if it is not what Ang wants or values. But if he really loves to vacuum and wants to be involved, then he will have to negotiate his way without assuming he has the right to it.

When you are considering your roles and who does which job, please also discuss skill sets. It is likely that if you have lived together for a long period then you will have developed skills in the areas that you have taken on as yours. I worked with a newly-widowed woman who did not know how to skype. Her husband had been the one who did anything to do with technology. Now she was unable to contact her adult children via skype at a time when she really needed them. I worked with a man who was a published and internationally acclaimed lecturer in his field. When his wife left him a year into retirement, he did not know how to turn on the oven. Admittedly, their oven was old and his wife had learned the tricks of getting it going and setting the temperature so that it did not burn everything to a crisp, but he was still well short of being able to use it when he couldn't even turn it on! Make sure you start to multi-skill. Even if you don't think you are going to be the one responsible for the role, make sure you know how to do it.

<hr>

TASK: Clarifying roles

Make three lists titled as follows:
- Your jobs
- My jobs
- Our jobs

Work separately to brainstorm the jobs that each of you do. Simply list the jobs under each heading.

REFLECTION

Share your lists with your partner once you have developed them. Rather than coming up with a prescriptive list of who does what, you might try to make this conversation a springboard for deeper discussion.

Perhaps ask each other:
- Is our previous division of labour still working for us?
- What would you like us to do differently?
- Why do you think that xxx is my job?
- Why do you think that xxx is your job?
- Has your experience while growing up influenced your expectations about who does what?

When your retirement or that of your partner is not voluntary or planned

This can be an emotional roller coaster. Even if the person who has been jettisoned into retirement can see many positives in the situation, no-one likes to feel that they are not in control of their life. It is also a very disappointing way to finish a work life. Such a situation can bring about a period of grieving.

Grieving happens in response to a situation of loss. Loss happens when a person is made redundant or is forced, for reasons such as health, to suddenly retire. The losses include loss of control, predictability, money, financial freedom, identity, pride, structure, purpose, meaning, and status.

Grieving is not a predictable journey. It affects people differently. Some people will go into denial. 'Sure, I may have to leave this job, but I will get another one soon enough. I just have to start looking and bring in all my contacts.' Or, 'No, I am not upset. Why do you keep harping on at me?' Or, 'I am glad to be out of a job. I was over that company anyway. Good riddance'. Some people will become angry or irritable. 'Where are my car keys? This house is a mess. Do I have to do everything around here?' Many people will experience fear.

'What am I going to do? How will I tell the kids? What will I say to our friends?' Some fear is hard to put into words, such as the fear of, 'Who will I be now?'

Most people slip in and out of these emotions with periods of feeling calm in between. For more information, turn to *Chapter 16: A bend in the road is not the end of the road* which deals with a retirement that is not of your choosing, and to *Chapter 17: The happiness hijackers* which deals with issues such as depression and anxiety.

While it is hard for the person who has been made redundant or who has been retired unexpectedly, it is also very hard for that person's partner. Of course, some partners might be thrilled that their partner has finally been forced to retire. As Jennie said to me, 'At last! There is no way he would have retired if it was left up to him. But he is 70 for heaven's sake. I want to relax and enjoy our lives but that won't happen for a while even though he has now officially retired. He is going to be like a bear with a sore head'.

But if the bear's head AND heart are very sore, it is a difficult challenge for the partner. It is hard to support a person who is variously calm, angry, accepting, scared, and perhaps avoidant. Not only is the partner trying to offer care to someone who is struggling, but the newly-retired partner also has to deal with his or her own loss and experience of sudden change. They may also experience loss of control, predictability, money, financial freedom, identity, pride, structure, purpose, meaning, and status.

Loss and grief

The information below may immediately have relevance for you – or not. If not, please read it anyway and consider where it might relate in your life. Few people get to retirement age without suffering some loss. Sometimes we can get stuck in dealing with a loss and it stays with us, becoming part of the fabric of our being. In this way it continues to impact on us, on our partner, and on our relationship.

You may be familiar with the idea that there are stages of grieving. This idea was introduced by Dr Elisabeth Kübler-

Ross in 1969.[i] She was a Swiss psychiatrist who worked in palliative care. There are several stages that a grieving person may experience. These stages do not occur in a set order, and some people will experience only a few of the stages while others might experience all of them. Some people may experience a particular stage over a period of weeks or months, while for others it may be fleeting.

There are considered to be up to seven stages of grief. They include shock, denial, anger, guilt/bargaining, depression, testing, and acceptance. Remember this is not a set list, nor is there any prescribed order.

- Shock. This is a very understandable emotion when life changes suddenly. You might feel numb.

- Denial. If the change is a negative one, we often seek a way to deny the change. You may feel as if your brain cannot take in the information and you are left wondering, 'How can it be? Surely someone has given me the wrong information!'

- Anger. Fear is often masked by anger. You may find yourself claiming the situation is unfair, unreasonable, and underserved, and asking why.

- Guilt and Bargaining. You may look for someone to blame or blame yourself. You may find yourself asking:
  - Where did I go wrong?
  - Is it my fault? Am I to blame?
  - If only I hadn't …
  - If only he had …

  You may look for a way out of the situation, thinking:
  - What if I do something differently now?
  - If I change, can I change it?

- Depression. You may experience feelings of emptiness and despair as the reality settles in. Sadness can be overwhelming when the full impact of loss is felt.

- Testing. This stage is about moving towards acceptance. It is marked by looking for realistic options and solutions and ways of moving forward.

- Acceptance. Acceptance does not mean that you are happy with the situation. It means only that you feel calmer, have accepted the reality of what is, and have found a way to begin the journey forward.

TASK: Identifying whether you are in a stage of grieving

Consider the stages described above and assess whether you or your partner maybe in one of them.

REFLECTION

If you feel that you, or anyone else in your life who has been affected by your unplanned retirement, is stuck in one of these stages, then I strongly suggest that you source psychological help. The earlier you act, the easier it is to resolve the problem.

In this chapter and in the previous one we have explored the skills of talking together and sharing, developed an understanding your conflict style and the concept of role specificity, gained an understanding of relationship phases, and considered the impact of loss and grief. This combination of information and skill building will help to protect your toes while you listen to the music and find a new dance!

---

[i] Kübler-Ross, E. (1969). *On death and dying.* New York: The Macmillan Company.

Chapter 16.

A bend in the road is not the end of the road: When retirement was not of your choosing

Retirement is a stage that does not always begin as expected or as planned. If you are facing a retirement that is not of your choice, you may have a number of challenges to overcome in order to truly enjoy and engage with this part of your life. Those who have been thrust unexpectedly, or unwillingly, into retirement seem to be the ones most likely to suffer with depression or anxiety. Longhurst's research[i] supported earlier studies and showed that 'retirees who had retired voluntarily experienced significantly lower levels of stress, anxiety, depression and bad health than those who were forced to retire'. If you fall into the forced-retirement group, it is important to take extra care. Being informed, understanding your own emotional state, and having insight and skill is highly protective. You have read the previous chapter on the impact of involuntary retirement on your relationship, and will find more detailed information in *Chapter 17: The happiness hijackers* which deals with psychological conditions in more depth.

Of course, not everyone will be unhappy to be forced into retirement. Some people will be relieved to have the decision made for them. Some may see it as a get-out-of-jail card that enables them to leave without guilt. Some will have manoeuvred carefully to obtain a forced retirement. Some, while happy to enter retirement, will struggle with the manner in which it came about.

An American organisation, the Employee Benefit Research Institute (EBRI) does research into retirement.[ii] According to the 2015 EBRI Retirement Confidence Survey:

> *... many Americans find themselves retiring unexpectedly. The RCS [Retirement Confidence Survey] has consistently found that a large percentage of retirees leave the workforce earlier than planned (50 percent in 2015). Many retirees who retired earlier than planned cite hardships for leaving the workforce when they did, including health problems or disability (60 percent), changes at their company, such as downsizing or closure (27 percent), and having to care for a spouse or another family member (22 percent)*
>
> *...*

When Craig was made redundant, he expressed nothing but resentment and anger towards the company where he had been employed for 16 years. He was consumed with legal aspects of his company's actions in making him redundant and of a previous failure of promotion that preceded his redundancy. Underneath his anger was fear. His anger helped him to avoid feelings of anxiety and the many questions around his future, such as, would he be able to get a new job, or should he just retire? Could he afford to retire? He preferred instead to dwell on the mismanagement perpetrated on him by his boss and his company.

Brenda worked as an emergency nurse, three days a week, until she was forced to resign when diagnosed with bowel cancer. She coped well with her treatment and was told she was in remission. Brenda was fearful of trying to return to work. She was 54. Most of her fear was grounded in her underlying belief that the stress of work contributed to her getting cancer. Brenda felt that for the sake of her health she must retire.

Lance was forced into an earlier-than-expected retirement when he caught his arm in a piece of machinery on the factory floor. Lance had many months of rehabilitation on his arm. During that time, he did not know how much use of his right arm he would ultimately regain. Lance's wife was devastated by his injury. She cried frequently and moved between anger and anxiety. She spent hours on the internet searching for medical interventions that might assist or, as Lance said, provide some sort of miracle. There was little opportunity for Lance to allow himself to feel his own feelings while he tried to deal with his wife's emotions.

Craig, Brenda and Lance, like most people faced with an earlier-than-anticipated retirement, had more to think about than just retiring. There can be an overwhelming number of losses, plus accompanying major demands such as legal issues, claims administration, hospital paperwork, the emotions of other people, and the many unknowns. These all combine to make a forced retirement very difficult.

In this chapter I want to focus on making a distinction between the events that lead you into a forced retirement and retirement as you are experiencing it. It is easy to lose your way in the maelstrom of dealing with:

- the event that precipitated retirement
- the myriad of events that have followed
- your own emotions
- the emotions of the people around you.

There is a danger that the act of retiring can be thrust, unthinkingly, into your bag of bad things that are happening and over which you have no control.

TASK: Sorting the experience of forced retirement from its cause

Complete the following statements.

1. *The event that pushed me into early retirement was:*

....

....

....

2. Because of that event I have lost:

....

....

....

3. Because of that event I have gained:

....

....

....

4. How I feel about a) the event that resulted in my retirement and b) how I feel about being retired:

....

....

....

You might want to use the list of words at the end of this chapter to help you to describe how you feel. You might like to use two highlighters. With one colour, highlight the words that describe how you feel about the event that caused your retirement, and with the second colour, highlight the words that describe how you feel about being retired.

REFLECTION

Compare your list of gains (positives) and losses (negatives). Do the losses relate to retirement or to the event? What about the gains? Then compare your two lists of emotions regarding how you feel about the event and how you feel about retiring. Is there something you need to let go of in order to enjoy the retirement phase of your life?

When Craig completed this part of the task, he already knew that he felt anger and resentment because of the event (his redundancy), but he had not recognised the fear. And with regards to retiring, he had not realised that he was feeling shame. He immediately understood that he would have to let go of this shame if he were to enjoy his days in retirement.

Brenda was conscious of her anxiety about her illness (the event). She was not aware, until she completed the exercise, that she was actually optimistic about retiring.

When Lance did the task, he realised that his losses related to how he felt about his new disability, rather than to retiring.

Emotions: yours or others

Just as your unplanned retirement is likely to impact on you emotionally, it may also impact on other people in your life. Lance's wife had a history of depression and anxiety. It was well controlled until Lance was injured. She began to have panic attacks as well as experiencing an ongoing low mood. Lance was beset by guilt and worry about his wife. It is important to separate your emotions from those of the people around you and to take the time to deal with your own emotions.

According to the results of the EBRI Retirement Confidence Survey, health problems, disability, job loss, and job changes are the major contributors to forced retirement. These factors are easily identified as ones likely to cause significant life upheaval and loss. Loss can lead to grief. Grieving can lead to sadness, to anxiety, to fear, to anger, and sometimes to depression. Grief is an important and sometimes unrecognised part of a forced retirement. There is grief for the multiple losses sustained. This grief can go unnamed and unrecognised because it is overwhelmed by the more obvious factors, such as a newly acquired disability or financial fears. In my experience, grief is one of the primary emotions underlying a forced retirement. Have a read of the preceding chapter where I have described the stages of grief if you have not yet done so.

One of the more disturbing types of loss, that can be hard to identify, is a sense that you have lost control of your life. If life can do *this* to you, what else might it do? Suddenly life is filled with unknowns. This sense of vulnerability is frightening. Sometimes the fear is obscured by anger towards whatever seems to have wrenched control out of your hands. Often there is also expected or predicted loss that compounds the real loss. At times this anticipatory loss can be more powerful than the actual loss. As we all know, it is easier to deal with facts than waiting and what if-ing the unknowns. Thinking is a potentially dangerous game. We spend hours each day talking to ourselves and listening to ourselves as though what we are saying is very important and worthwhile, when in fact it is often fear-driven drivel.

Nietzsche, a famous and influential German philosopher in the mid to late 1800s said, 'thoughts are the shadows of our feelings – always darker emptier and simpler'.[iii] It seems arrogant of me to disagree with a famous and erudite philosopher (especially as we are not at the pub having a beer where I know I can out-erudite anyone), but I do disagree with his claim that thoughts are the shadows of our feelings. I believe that feelings are the shadows of our thoughts. It is our dark thoughts made simple by black and white or all-encompassing erroneous statements, such as, 'I am always making mistakes', or, 'I am never going to lose weight', that create our feelings. Negative thoughts lead to negative feelings and positive thoughts create positive feelings.

Our lives are constantly changing and we, in response, are constantly evolving. It is at times like this, when much is being asked of us, that our freedom to choose can add to the burden of demands that we are facing. We are not just facing a choice of which action to take. We are faced with the difficult choices which ask, who I will be? Nietzsche, the same German philosopher, said in 1888[iv] that 'if we have our own why in life, we shall get along with almost any how'. And this time, I agree with him!

In the coming chapters we will explore in more detail the psychological conditions that take from our ability to enjoy happiness.

---

[i] Longhurst, M. (2018). Enjoying retirement: An Australian handbook of ideas, strategies and resources. Sydney: Hachette Australia.

[ii] Helman, R., Copeland, C., & VanDerhei, J. (2015). 'The 2015 retirement confidence survey: Having a retirement savings plan a key factor in Americans' retirement confidence'. *EBRI Issue Brief,* *413*(26), 26-27. Retrieved from http://www.ebri.org/pdf/surveys/rcs/2015/EBRI_IB_413_Apr15_RCS-2015.pdf.

[iii] Nietzsche, F.W. (1882). *Die fröhliche Wissenschaft.* Chemnitz: Ernst Schmeitzner.

[iv] Nietzsche, F. (1888). Götzen-Dämmerung: oder Wie man mit dem Hammer philosophiert. Leipzig: C.G. Naumann.

Chapter 17.

The happiness hijackers: Depression, anxiety, stress and anger

Depression, anxiety, stress, and anger are thieves that can perform a happiness hijack at any time in your life, including in your retirement. You may experience one of these villains acting alone, or a cluster of them, or even all of them, as they tend to hold hands and travel as a pack. You may not be able to put a name to what you are experiencing, so let's look in more detail at what they are and how they relate to each other.

Depression

Depression is more than feeling down. Typical signs and symptoms of depression include:

- a low mood most of the day and nearly every day
- sleep problems such as difficulty getting to sleep, waking during the night, often with difficulty getting back to sleep, or early waking
- a change in appetite – eating too much or too little. A weight change of more than 5% is noteworthy
- loss of motivation
- feelings of worthlessness, guilt or hopelessness
- difficulty making decisions, concentrating or remembering
- not finding pleasure in things that usually would bring pleasure or interest

- feeling tired for no reason
- increased tearfulness, irritability or anger
- feeling agitated and unable to sit still or alternatively feeling unable to get moving
- recurrent thoughts of death.

This is the typical smorgasbord of depressive symptoms. People with depression can experience some or all, and with varying intensity. Most people, even those who are not depressed, have experienced some of these symptoms at some time in their lives. The difference is the number of symptoms experienced, the unrelenting nature of those symptoms, and their level of impact on the person's day-to-day functioning.

Kathleen retired when the company where she had worked for ten years closed down. She had felt ready to retire. Her main concern in life was her daughter's marriage. She was worried about it and about her daughter's future. But this situation had not changed in the last five years. Kathleen's husband had left her nine years previously. Kathleen felt that she had worked through the grief of the separation. Once retired, she noticed that the house was silent and she felt alone. She began having difficulty getting to sleep. As a result, she started going to bed later and sleeping later. She could not seem to find the motivation to go out, so she began eating more and watching TV. She found herself crying over TV dramas. Increasingly, she thought about her own failed marriage and wondered if it was her fault. Then she began thinking repeatedly about her daughter's situation. Were her daughter's marital problems a result of being the child of separated parents? Perhaps it was her fault? She felt down-hearted and without direction. Kathleen felt like a failure.

The road to depression can be a slippery one and Kathleen appeared to be on such a road. A low mood which does not go away should raise an alarm. The longer you leave depression untreated, the harder it can be to treat.

Sometimes grief can look very like depression. The letting-go process can be akin to a grieving process. If you believe that you may be depressed, then it will be worthwhile arranging to see a psychologist for a check-up.

Anxiety

Anxiety is more than feeling stressed. Anxiety is something of an umbrella term. There are many anxiety disorders, such as generalised anxiety disorder, agoraphobia, social anxiety disorder, and panic disorder.

Most people are aware of the physical signs of anxiety. Typical physical signs and symptoms of anxiety include:

- heart racing or palpitations
- feeling short of breath or over breathing
- dizziness
- butterflies in the stomach
- tightness or pain in the chest
- sweating
- clamminess
- fatigue
- diarrhoea
- blushing
- headaches
- tight muscles.

There are also psychological signs which include:

- excessive worrying or obsessing
- a sense of gloom and doom about the future
- procrastination
- perfectionism or high expectations
- mind racing – often in bed, which disrupts sleep
- fuzzy thinking and recall.

Henry was a well-dressed man in his late 60s. His wife had died some years previously. Her death was long and painful, and Henry had nursed her lovingly. Now Henry was ready to retire. He had met a woman to whom he was attracted. They had a lot in common and enjoyed each other's company. Adele had suggested to Henry that once he retired, she accompany him on an extended caravanning trip. This seemed like a good idea to Henry. However, when they began to make plans for the trip, Henry began to wonder if he was doing the right thing, both about retiring and travelling with Adele. He began to have chest pain, periodic shortness of breath, and a feeling of dizziness. Henry began to worry obsessively about his health even though his doctor did exhaustive testing and assured him that his heart was in good shape. His symptoms became worse the more Henry worried. Henry came to see me shortly before his retirement. Fortunately, he was quickly able to grasp the impact of his thoughts on his physical state and the physiological facts that produce anxiety symptoms. He learned strategies to manage both his physical symptoms and his thoughts, and I received a post card from the Kimberley, in Western Australia, some months later.

Change makes most people anxious. Retirement is a significant life change. Anxiety has a profoundly negative impact on quality of life. Yet, it is one of the conditions that responds well to simple strategies that are easy to learn. If you think you might have anxiety, or you are aware of a sense of nervousness that is uncomfortable, intense or prolonged, seek professional advice from a psychologist who will be able to provide prompt assistance to halt a downward spiral and get you back on track.

Depression and anxiety together

Depression and anxiety are known as co-morbid conditions. I recall my shock when I first learned of co-morbidity while still a student of psychology. I thought it meant that together they could kill a person. I was vastly relieved to learn that co-morbidity simply means that the two conditions tend to occur together. Depression and generalised anxiety disorder are co-morbid about 50% of the time. This statistic is found in a book titled *The Anxious Brain* by S. Prinz and M. Wehrenberg.[i] In this excellent book the authors make the point that the co-morbidity may be due to the person's brain state when depression is the primary, or first occurring condition, and anxiety develops subsequently. When the development of the comorbidity is reversed, it is possible that the depression may be the understandable result of having a debilitating condition of anxiety.

Stress

Stress has been well researched and much discussed as a burden of our modern lifestyle with its enormous financial and social pressures. But in our society, having stress is also considered a validation that you are living life to the full. Stress is known to be implicated as causal in both physical and mental health conditions. Stress impacts on the brain and makes it more vulnerable to anxiety, depression, and reactivity such as anger.

Symptoms of stress include:
- change of appetite and/or sleep
- repetitive habits or movements such as fiddling, nail biting, teeth grinding, pacing
- low immunity
- problems such as headaches, stomach problems, skin problems
- lowered libido
- fatigue
- loss of humour
- taking comments personally
- startling easily
- physical signs such as those experienced in anxiety.

Kyle came to see me because he was having angry outbursts. His doctor thought the anger might be stress related. Kyle was a very busy father whose focus was on earning money by having two jobs, finding time to be the soccer coach for his son's team, and renovating the family home so it could be put up for sale to cover existing debts. Kyle accepted this range of stress-inducing activities as normal. He believed his stress was coming from his marriage. According to Kyle, his wife was 'not making space for him'. He was angry with her and depressed by the state of his marriage. It took some time before Kyle accepted that his mood and reactivity were more about his chronic stress than his wife and marriage. His anger and bleak moods resolved once we addressed the source of his stress.

Anger

Anger is often considered a secondary emotion. A secondary emotion is one we move into in order to protect ourselves from another emotion. We do not do this consciously. It is a self-protective mechanism. Many people are more comfortable with the energy that anger provides, rather than feeling the helplessness of grief or fear. This energy can restore a sense of power and control, even if it is illusory. The problem with this self-protective mechanism is that it is not known to the person who is experiencing the anger. The angry person who invests in the anger and justifies it will find it hard to let it go. As a result, the other emotion remains hidden and active.

Anger may be:
- chronic; constant feelings of anger that are overt or held in
- passive; which can appear as sullenness, lack of co-operation, blaming of others
- short lived
- sudden and uncontrollable
- violent, such as hitting a wall.

Characteristics of anger include:
- difficulty in calming down
- having a big response to a small problem
- having a need for substances
- physical signs, such as those experienced in anxiety.

Anger depression and anxiety

Depression has been described as unexpressed anger. This is a large generalisation and it does not apply to all depressions, but it has some validity. Anxiety and anger are sometimes fellow travellers. When a person has been in a state of heightened arousal due to anxiety, they are likely to blow up when just one more thing is added to the mix. Interestingly, anxiety and anger are often difficult for a person to differentiate. If you have had an upbringing where anger was disallowed, or you lived in a situation where it was not safe to express anger, then you may have difficulty telling the difference between anxiety and anger.

Emily was referred to me for anxiety. She was a self-effacing woman and always ready to apologise – even if it was not her fault. Her father had been a tyrant and her mother a pleaser. Emily's last bout of overt anger occurred when she was in her late teens and it scared her. She was so angry that she lost control and hit her mother with a metal pipe. She was confused that her anger was towards her inoffensive mother and not her controlling father. Emily felt upset and nervous just recalling the event from 50 years previously. Since that time her anger had become passively expressed. Her family thought of her as withdrawn, unfriendly, and difficult. In therapy we got to the point where Emily could feel anger rather than anxiety. Next, she experienced the anger so intensely that she felt it would overwhelm her. Once she allowed the anger to burn, openly and safely, both her anxiety and her anger diminished significantly. She was then able to differentiate when she was angry and when she was anxious and to react accordingly.

TASK: Assessing your own mental health state

Go back to the symptoms of depression, anxiety, stress, and anger outlined in this chapter. Use a highlighter to mark symptoms that you may have.

REFLECTION

The lists of symptoms are not conclusive. Many of the symptoms of the conditions of depression, anxiety, stress, and anger overlap. If you have more than three in any group, try discussing your situation with your doctor or a psychologist, or with someone you trust to give you an honest response.

---

[i] Prinz. S., & Wehrenberg, M. (2007). The anxious brain: The neurobiological basis of anxiety disorders and how to effectively treat them. New York: W.W. Norton & Company.

Chapter 18.

Happiness, life satisfaction, and wellbeing: How to make it yours

Happiness

The work that you have completed so far in this book has been directed towards developing a healthy self-identity, maintaining currency and relevancy, growing a portfolio of interests, and creating a vision for your retirement. This mix of factors is a good recipe for happiness during your retirement phase. But when we speak of happiness, are we talking about the 'woohoo' happiness that flares and dies like fireworks, or the happiness of contentment and wellbeing? One is called hedonic happiness and the other eudemonic happiness. Hedonic happiness is the one where feelings are of pleasure. Unfortunately, these feelings are brief and often intense, but are also fleeting and unsustainable. Eudemonic happiness is less intense but longer lasting. Eudemonic refers to a happiness linked to having a sense of purpose and meaning. It leads to life satisfaction and personal wellbeing.

Hedonic happiness is generally a result of things outside of yourself; having a good time with others, buying something, eating a delicious food. You feel good when something MAKES you feel happy. Eudemonic happiness, while allowing for moments of hedonic happiness, comes from a life based on purpose and meaning. We tend not to differentiate between hedonic happiness and eudemonic happiness, but it is important to do so. Often, we seek hedonic (pleasure) happiness, mistakenly thinking it will lead to eudemonic (purpose and meaning) happiness.

For many people, their work provides a sense of purpose and productivity, and both are important sources of eudemonic happiness. If your source of eudemonic happiness is, or was, your work, it will disappear when your work does. If you have been a worker who always gives 110%, how will you turn off the spotlight after a lifetime of work hyper-focus? And what will you replace it with when you go into retirement?

Work can also provide a sense of community, another important source of eudemonic happiness. This sense of belonging to a group with a common purpose is often lost in retirement. The importance of community on happiness is highlighted in the World Happiness report of 2015 which makes a comparison between money and connection to others, in terms of capacity to influence happiness. It states that 'studies have shown that a sense of belonging to community has the same effect on life satisfaction as trebling of household income'.[i]

I had a colleague who worked as a counsellor with drug and alcohol users. She was a wonderful practitioner and generous with her time and expertise to both clients and her colleagues. When Annie retired, some years ago, we gave her a great send off. No-one deserved a good retirement more than she did. Yet, after a seemingly brief period of hedonistic activity (travel, redecorating the house, and going for coffee), she found her life to be empty and meaningless. For Annie, hedonistic activity could not match the sense of purpose she had obtained through her intense work focus. Nor could the eudemonic happiness of connection found in her work be replaced by moments of hedonic happiness. Atchley,[ii] a sociologist researching retirement in the 1970s, described a honeymoon phase where 'the retirement event is often followed by a rather euphoric period … ' This euphoric period that Atchley describes is the period of hedonic happiness. He goes on to identify the disenchantment phase, just as Annie experienced.

Annie is typical of many people who have a belief that life will be wonderful when they retire, because they will finally have time to do all those things they have not had time for while working. There will be an initial period of freedom and a sense of pleasure, but this is likely to be followed by a sense of emptiness and loss. Usually the initial activities are hedonistic. Remember, in this context hedonistic is not bad or wrong or overly indulgent. It is a source of happiness that we need in our lives. It comes from sources outside of ourselves and creates a sense of pleasure. But it must be balanced. It is essential to ensure that you have a balance of eudemonic and hedonic happiness in your life, with resulting life satisfaction and psychological wellbeing.

Now we have explored happiness, we will next look at the concepts of life satisfaction and wellbeing. Life satisfaction is different to happiness and to wellbeing. Life satisfaction is not about feelings; rather, it is an assessment of one's life, as a whole. Psychological wellbeing is a more encompassing term, and indicates that the person has achieved, not happiness, but a happiness balance. Psychologists tend now to talk of wellbeing rather than happiness. There is no agreed textbook definition of wellbeing, but happiness, both eudemonic and hedonic, and life satisfaction are necessary parts of wellbeing.

Psychological wellbeing is important: not just for quality of life, but also quantity. An article published in *The Lancet* on 5 November 2014 stated that 'the English Longitudinal Study of Ageing, identified that eudemonic wellbeing is associated with increased survival; ... Associations were independent of age, sex, demographic factors, and baseline mental and physical health'. [iii]

Life satisfaction

An expert in this area is Ed Diener, psychologist, professor, and author. He co-created the Satisfaction With Life Scale.[iv] It has been reproduced here, with his permission, and you might like to complete it.

TASK: Completing the Satisfaction With Life Scale

Below are five statements. Using the 1 – 7 scale below, indicate your agreement with each item.

7	6	5	4	3	2	1
Strongly agree	Agree	Slightly agree	Neither agree nor disagree	Slightly disagree	Disagree	Strongly disagree

In most ways my life is close to my ideal.	
The conditions of my life are excellent.	
I am satisfied with my life.	
So far, I have gotten the important things I want in life.	
If I could live my life over, I would change almost nothing.	

Find the sum of your scores and identify where you are placed.

31 – 35	26 – 30	21 – 25	20	15 – 19	10 – 14	5 – 9
Extremely satisfied	Satisfied	Slightly satisfied	Neutral	Slightly dissatisfied	Dis-satisfied	Extremely dissatisfied

REFLECTION

Think about why you achieved your score.

- *If you had completed this task early in your life would the result have been different? Why?*
- *Did one area pull down your Total? What was it?*
- *If you complete this task in the near future, do you predict that something will have changed? Why?*
- *Is there something you need to address to move your score upwards?*

Following are Diener's notes on each score category.

30 – 35 Very high score. *Highly satisfied respondents who score in this range love their lives and feel that things are going very well. Their lives are not perfect, but they feel that things are about as good as lives get. Furthermore, just because the person is satisfied does not mean she or he is complacent. In fact, growth and challenge might be part of the reason the respondent is satisfied. For most people in this high-scoring range, life is enjoyable, and the major domains of life are going well – work or school, family, friends, leisure, and personal development.*

25- 29 High score. *Individuals who score in this range like their lives and feel that things are going well. Of course, their lives are not perfect, but they feel that things are mostly good. Furthermore, just because the person is satisfied does not mean she or he is complacent. In fact, growth and challenge might be part of the reason the respondent is satisfied. For most people in this high-scoring range, life is enjoyable, and the major domains of life are going well – work or school, family, friends, leisure, and personal development. The person may draw motivation from the areas of dissatisfaction.*

20-24 Average score. *The average of life satisfaction in economically developed nations is in this range – the majority of people are generally satisfied, but have some areas where they very much would like some improvement. Some individuals score in this range because they are mostly satisfied with most areas of their lives but see the need for some improvement in each area. Other respondents score in this range because they are satisfied with most domains of their lives, but have one or two areas where they would like to see large improvements. A person scoring in this range is normal in that they have areas of their lives that need improvement. However, an individual in this range would usually like to move to a higher level by making some life changes.*

15 – 19 Slightly below average score. *People who score in this range usually have small but significant problems in several areas of their lives, or have many areas that are doing fine but one area that represents a substantial problem for them. If a person has moved temporarily into this level of life satisfaction from a higher level because of some recent event, things will usually improve over time and satisfaction will generally move back up. On the other hand, if a person is chronically slightly dissatisfied with many areas of life, some changes might be in order. Sometimes the person is simply expecting* *too much, and sometimes life changes are needed. Thus, although temporary dissatisfaction is common and normal, a chronic level of dissatisfaction across a number of areas of life calls for reflection. Some people can gain motivation from a small level of dissatisfaction, but often dissatisfaction across a number of life domains is a distraction, and unpleasant as well.*

__10 – 14 Low score.__ Dissatisfied people who score in this range are substantially dissatisfied with their lives. People in this range may have a number of domains that are not going well, or one or two domains that are going very badly. If life dissatisfaction is a response to a recent event such as bereavement, divorce, or a significant problem at work, the person will probably return over time to his or her former level of higher satisfaction. However, if low levels of life satisfaction have been chronic for the person, some changes are in order – both in attitudes and patterns of thinking, and probably in life activities as well. Low levels of life satisfaction in this range, if they persist, can indicate that things are going badly and life alterations are needed. Furthermore, a person with low life satisfaction in this range is sometimes not functioning well because their unhappiness serves as a distraction. Talking to a friend, member of the clergy, counsellor, or other specialist can often help the person get moving in the right direction, although positive change will be up to the person.

__5 – 9 Very low score.__ Extremely dissatisfied individuals who score in this range are usually extremely unhappy with their current life. In some cases, this is in reaction to some recent bad event such as widowhood or unemployment. In other cases, it is a response to a chronic problem such as alcoholism or addiction. In yet other cases, the extreme dissatisfaction is a reaction due to something bad in life such as recently having lost a loved one. However, dissatisfaction at this level is often due to dissatisfaction in multiple areas of life. Whatever the reason for the low level of life satisfaction, it may be that the help of others is needed – a friend or family member, counselling with a member of the clergy, or help from a psychologist or other counsellor. If the dissatisfaction is chronic, the person needs to change, and often others can help.

It is interesting to identify your current level of life satisfaction, but it is much more important to act to improve your score. Life satisfaction is a key criterion, and an essential component, of a successful retirement.

Wellbeing

Professor Martin Seligman, a pioneer in the area of positive psychology and former head of the American Psychological Association, has identified the contributing factors in life satisfaction and the resulting wellbeing. His model is called PERMA.[v] PERMA is an acronym for the five factors which all contribute to wellbeing. They are:

- **P**ositive emotions – feeling good, happy, alive
- **E**ngagement – losing yourself in an activity, being absorbed in the present, doing productive and meaningful activity
- **R**elationships – being connected to others, having a network or community, able to be yourself with others
- **M**eaning – a purposeful existence which links us to something greater than ourselves, living in a way that is consistent with our own values and beliefs
- **A**ccomplishment – a sense of personal success, meeting of goals.

By reading this book you have already engaged in exploring and developing yourself in each of these areas.

Energy tanks

I want to take you one further step to ensuring your wellbeing and the creation of a satisfying life. I would like you to explore your energy tanks. Imagine that you have a series of energy tanks powering your life. When these tanks are full of fuel you will have the energy to create and achieve wellbeing and a satisfying life. Each tank needs to have a little bit in it to power your life successfully. You might think of it as being like a complex car that has seven fuel tanks. Running the car on only one or two or three tanks will damage the car in the long term. The car works best when each tank has fuel in it. I have related each tank to one of the PERMA factors, and, as you will see, some tanks contribute to more than one factor.

The 7 Tanks:

1. Physical: your body, your health, and your energy.
   (**E**ngagement, **P**ositive emotions, **A**ccomplishment)
2. Intellectual: stimulation and learning. It does not have to be difficult learning but rather something that gets you thinking.
   (**E**ngagement, **A**ccomplishment)
3. Social: belonging or connection with other people or a group.
   (**R**elationships)
4. Giving: of your time or money or your skills or of yourself in some way.
   (**M**eaning, **R**elationships)
5. Creativity: expressing yourself in a creative way.
   (**A**ccomplishment)
6. Spirituality: connection with something bigger then yourself.
   (**M**eaning)
7. Wellbeing: feeling good, contented, satisfied with life.
   (**P**ositive emotions, **R**elationships)

The choices you make each day provide an opportunity for tank filling. For example, you will give your social tank a top-up if you go to an enjoyable social event where you meet your friends. You can fill tanks simultaneously. If you undertake a course of study in a photography class you are likely to add fuel to the intellectual, creative, and social tanks.

Karen was a kindergarten teacher. She had never married and had no children. She assessed her energy tanks and the fuel in each.

She assessed her physical tank as being 80% full. She felt fit and energetic. She did yoga daily and weekly fitness classes. Intellectual was 95%. Karen was completing her Master's degree and felt fully engaged in it. Her social tank was another surprise. It was at 40% even though she had a loving extended family and good friends. The giving tank was at 50% as Karen felt she gave a lot to the children in her care, but she identified her giving was limited to work. Her creativity was assessed at

30% for the same reason. Spiritual was at 90% and this reflected Karen's yoga and meditation. Wellbeing was rated at 50%. Using the information from completing this exercise, Karen and I were able to quickly identify the changes she needed to make to improve her wellbeing.

TASK: Checking the fuel levels

Physical   Intellectual   Social   Giving
Creativity   Spiritual   Wellbeing

Draw seven tall, rectangular tanks. On the vertical axis add a scale from 0 to 100, marking off 10, 20, 30, etc. all the way up to 100. On the horizontal axis write the name of each tank.

Think about each tank. You need to gauge how full each one is. If it is full you will make a mark at 100. If it is half-full mark it at 50 and so on. Most people are able to do this with surprising speed and accuracy. Just make a mark where you think it is. Do it in pencil as you might want to adjust the level as you complete the task. Sometimes the level of a tank changes when you think about it relative to the other tanks.

REFLECTION

How full is each tank for you? Too full? Not full enough? Just right? What do you need to do differently?

In the next chapter we will consider each tank and explore ways of refilling and refuelling yourself.

---

i http://worldhappiness.report/wp-content/uploads/sites/2/2015/04/WHR-2015-summary_final.pdf.

ii Atchley, R. C. (1976). *The sociology of retirement.* Cambridge, Massachusetts: Schenkman Pub. Co.

iii Steptoe, A., Deaton, A., & Stone, A. (2014). Subjective wellbeing, health, and ageing. *The Lancet, 385*(9968), 640-648. doi:10.1016/S0140-6736(13)61489-0.

iv Diener, E., Emmons, R.A., Larsen, R.J., & Griffin, S. (1985). The Satisfaction With Life Scale. *Journal of Personality Assessment, 49*(1), 71-75. doi: 10.1207/s15327752jpa4901_13.

v Seligman, M. (2011). Flourish: A visionary new understanding of happiness and well-being. New York: Free Press.

Chapter 19.

Fuelling your life: Filling your tanks

In this chapter we will discuss each of your energy tanks and how you can keep them topped up. Keep your completed tank diagram from the previous chapter close by. If you have a partner, it will be interesting to compare your tanks.

The physical tank

The physical tank is often the easiest to fill. But it is important to fill it with good quality fuel. Many people try to fill this tank with comfort foods or drinks. However, this tank is really about honouring your body. How well have you fed, watered, and exercised it? If you treated your pet pooch the same way as you treat your body, would it be thriving?

If this tank is low, what will you do to replenish it? Exercise is enormously important to our wellbeing. Increasingly, there is neurological evidence to help us to understand why exercise is so helpful. Here is the neurobiological background that will help you to make sense of it. Let me introduce you to brain derived neurotrophic factor (BDNF), in case you have not already met. This is a protein that is produced in the brain and helps with the process of neurogenesis. Neurogenesis is the birth of new brain cells, commonly called neurons. Not all areas of the brain are capable of continuing to make new neurons throughout life, but some important areas are able to complete this feat. One of those areas is the hippocampus, which is responsible for memory and learning. It is also the part of the brain that shrinks when people have depression. In an article titled 'Depression, antidepressants and the shrinking hippocampus', author Robert Sapolsky[i] reports that major depression can cause atrophy (shrinkage) of up to 20% of the volume of the hippocampus. To age well, it is very important to maintain a healthy brain, especially the part of the brain that is critical for memory and learning. You don't want it to be shrinking! Now let's go back to BDNF. Ferris, Williams, and Shen,[ii] authors of an article titled 'The effect of acute exercise on serum brain-derived neurotrophic factor levels and cognitive function' concluded that 'BDNF levels in humans are significantly elevated in response to exercise, and the magnitude of increase is exercise intensity dependent'.

Of course, exercise does more than impact on BDNF. It also helps us to sleep better – and that is a very important contributor to good mental health. It is also thought to impact on the level of serotonin, a neurotransmitter. People with depression have low levels of serotonin.

There is a strong connection between anxiety and depression. They tend to occur together. Exercise helps to reduce the production of stress hormones of adrenaline and cortisol. And it stimulates the production of endorphins, which are another neurochemical ... a brain chemical that makes us feel good. Another great by-product of endorphins is that they act like an analgesic, reducing the perception of pain. They have been compared to having a morphine-like effect on the body.

So, if you want to stay brain healthy and fill the physical tank then start moving ... literally.

Another critical physical factor is diet. For example, there is a relationship between intake of simple carbohydrates and depression in older women. There is a huge amount of information, about diet and its relationship to depression and anxiety, available on the internet. I encourage you to seek it out and evaluate your diet.

Research is increasingly pointing to the essential role of gut flora on our emotional state. A book by Giulia Enders called *Gut: The inside story of our body's most under-rated organ*[iii] is a valuable resource. It is an easy read on the impact of gut flora on wellbeing. Giulia describes a piece of research she calls 'the forced swimming test'. Mice were put into a container of water and forced to swim or drown because their little feet could not touch the bottom. Some mice gave up easily and some continued to swim for their lives. Mice provided with bacteria to enhance gut function swam for longer, had less stress hormones in their blood, and performed better in learning and memory tests. A similar experiment on humans, who took gut enhancing bacteria for four weeks, showed change in the parts of the brain responsible for processing emotions and pain.

The intellectual tank

This is not so much about how your brain is working, but how much you are working your brain. How much stimulation are you getting? Are you being challenged to think? This is not the same as being stressed and having to get things done.

SallyAnn gave a typical answer to the question about how much was in this tank. She said, 'Well, my intellectual tank feels pretty empty, but I can't fit anything more in my head. It might not be intellectual, but I have to think about so many things. I have to make a list every day just to keep it in my head'. SallyAnn was right. This is not intellectual. She was referring to simple busyness.

What are you doing that challenges your brain in a stimulating way? Consider how frequently you are learning something new. Think about what you find engaging to ponder or discuss, and how often you are doing that in areas of interest to you. It does not have to be rigorous or academic.

The social tank

This is an important tank, as you have already learned. The social tank refers to your contact and relationships with others. You might have many friends yet be missing an intimate relationship. You might have a wonderful partner but not have enough friends. For some people, friends are enough. For others, an intimate other is enough. Most people want both. In this context, intimacy is about the closeness of a relationship rather than about sex or someone with whom you share the bathroom. Intimate relationships are ones where you are truly known by another person and where you can really be yourself. Sometimes a long-time old friend fills this role, or it can be filled by one of your adult children.

We need more than a partner or friendship, we also need to belong to a group or community. Many factors influence our level of need for social contact and relationships. Humans are social animals. We do best in a herd. This is not a choice. It is programmed into us for our survival. In the long-ago days of our early human history we had to exist within a group in order to be safe. We needed each other. We had to work together to meet needs of food, shelter, and protection. As a result, we are programmed to belong. When we do not have a sense of belonging, we are likely to name it as loneliness.

There are multiple studies on the effects of loneliness as we age. These studies have found that loneliness is associated with a reduced quality of life, poor subjective health, disability, increased use of social and health services, a higher risk of cognitive decline, and an increase in mortality. Finnish researchers have found that 'suffering from loneliness is common and indicates significant mortality risk in old age.'[iv]

We need connection to others through community and friendship. Look back to *Chapter 8: Finding direction*. Does it give you some ideas about filling your social tank?

The giving tank

How much and what are you giving? The idea of giving is not limited to giving of any specific nature. You might give money or time or your skills, but it is really about giving something of yourself, even if it is only a smile or a thank you. As we know, it is not what you get in life; rather, it is about what you do with what you get and what you give. We have no control over what we get, but we do have control over what we do and what we give. And choice and control make us feel good.

In an article titled 'It's good to be good: 2011 fifth annual scientific report on health, happiness and helping others', Stephen G Post wrote:[v]

> *This literature review presents an extensive set of scientific and medical studies regarding the benefits experienced by individuals who act sincerely for the benefit of others. Happiness, health and even longevity are benefits that have been reported in more than fifty investigations using a variety of methodologies ... The conclusion of this review is that when we help others, we help ourselves, with the caveat that we need balance in our lives and should not be overwhelmed.*

The World Happiness report 2015 states that 'it is interesting to observe that the effect of volunteering on life satisfaction is quantitatively the same as that of moving up by one decile in the income scale'.[vi]

Unfortunately, the results from the Australian Bureau of Statistics General Social Survey show continuing reductions in involvement in activities which connect people to their broader community, and the way people are interacting with the community outside their household, such as through volunteering.[vii]

In John Izzo's book, *The five secrets you must discover before you die,*[viii] he nominates one of the five secrets as to give more than you take. From a psychologist's perspective, this is a secret that needs to become common knowledge. It needs to be shouted from the rooftops until we, as a community and as individuals, hear and understand it. We are living in an increasingly individualistic society that puts the needs and wants of the individual before that of the group.

The evidence for the power of giving comes not just from psychological research. Brain research has shown that giving helps the giver. A 2016 paper[ix] reported how the act of giving support influenced the brain of the giver. fMRI technology made it possible for researchers to identify a positive impact of brain areas related to stress and threat, reward and caregiving.

Giving is a speedy way of filling more than one tank simultaneously. Perhaps part of the magic that results from giving is that it links us with something bigger than ourselves. When you give, it connects you to another person or group, or it supports something you believe in. Meaningful connections increase life satisfaction.

Penny was married to a successful builder and she worked hard in her husband's business doing the books, accounts, submitting tenders, and liaising with contractors. Her children went to expensive private schools and, as she worked in a family business, she was able to do the school runs in their late-model SUV. She dressed for the morning and afternoon run, often getting out of daggy home clothes to do so. The family outgoings did not always match the incoming money that had to support their lifestyle. Then, Penny's husband told her that he had been having an affair and that he was leaving to live with his new love. Of course, this was shattering. I met Penny two years later. She was working, maintaining the house as best she could, and keeping the children at their schools. Money was so tight that each week was an unknown. But she was relaxed and happy! I made an assumption that, as she became used to living without her husband, she had realised that she was happier without him. So many people seem to say this to me that I simply expected that Penny would also. But no. Penny said, 'I still miss my husband. I suppose I should not call him my husband; yet I still think of him as my husband, even though he is not. I miss so much about having a partner to share things with, someone to laugh with and someone to share the worries with'. I asked her if she was happier without him. The answer was no.

The next question I asked was, 'Why are you happy?' She said, 'I have wondered that myself. It has taken me two years to stop having real downs, but throughout that time I started to know serenity and contentment more than happiness. I noticed that I always felt better when I helped others. It was a physical thing. It would lift me out of myself in a way that nothing else did. Before my husband left, I would focus on the house and kids and keeping our busy social life in order. It felt good when I had a sparkling house and gave a lovely little dinner party where people had fun and were well fed and happy. I realise now that this was giving in a small way. But when my husband left, I started to do more. I began to do an hour of reading every Sunday at an aged care home. And I started to look for opportunities to be involved and to find ways to do little acts of giving. It might be really simple like letting someone go ahead of me in a queue. I don't know why it works, but it does for me'.

The creativity tank

'Creativity is inventing, experimenting, growing, taking risks, breaking rules, making mistakes, and having fun.' — Mary Lou Cook.

How can you fill your tank with creative juices and creative activity? How are you being creative in your life? Creativity is not limited to being an artist of some description. You might be a creative gardener or a creative cook. Most people find their creativity needs expression. It has to become something. What are you making or doing that expresses your creativity? Maya Angelou said, 'You can't use up creativity. The more you use, the more you have'.

So, what will you do to fill up your creativity tank? Don't take too long to do it, whatever it is. Simply DO something, while you are deliberating and mulling over your options. Do anything rather than nothing, even if it is finding a new recipe, replanting an area in the garden, or buying a colouring-in book and a set of pencils.

The spirituality tank

Would you call yourself a spiritual person? What does the word spiritual mean to you? Many people in our current Western cultures are wary of talking about spirituality. It smacks of religiosity. I supervise the practice of other psychologists. Almost invariably, when I ask my supervisee to tell me about their client's belief system, they do not know if their client has one. They do not know because they have not asked. They have not asked because they feel uncomfortable in doing so. Yet, they can happily ask their clients about their sex life and other highly personal information.

The doorway to spirituality is not confined to religion. Connection to and immersion in nature, creative endeavours such as writing, poetry, drawing, pottery, sculpting, woodwork and painting, meditation, and yogic practices are all portals to the spiritual experience. Being in love can create the experience of spirituality. A sense of connection with something greater than yourself is a means to the spiritual. Spirituality is uplifting. It is important to avail ourselves of such experiences and to allow ourselves the joy of it. No matter what the source of the experience, spirituality is calming and centring. It soothes and revitalises. Moments of spirituality and spiritual experience modify brain behaviour. If it is too low, what are you going to do to fill the tank?

The wellbeing tank

Is your wellbeing tank topped up with good-quality fuel and ready to provide the emotional energy you might require? Do you have the emotional reserves you might need if you hit a tough patch and you have to work hard to get through it? Or is your tank running close to empty? Perhaps it IS empty.

Just as with physical fitness, you can ask yourself, 'How emotionally fit am I?' Yet, it is a harder question to answer. You cannot test yourself. You cannot run for ten minutes and check your heart rate today and then reassess yourself next week as you can do to test your physical fitness.

So how do you assess your emotional fitness? Often, we are quite intuitive in answering this question. Think about how you have been coping over the last weeks. Think about how you feel facing each day when you wake up. Think about your motivation. Think about your sense of humour and your optimism. Consider whether you are noticing the prettiness of the day or if each day seems the same. Consider whether you are bouncing back easily from life's little frustrations and whether you are getting pleasure from things that should be giving you pleasure.

If this tank is low, what can you do to fill it up? Be aware of the relationship between your wellbeing tank and your physical tank. If both are low there may be a relationship between them.

Balance for life satisfaction

Now you understand the seven tanks and have identified which tanks you need to top up. The tanks do not need to have the same amount in each, but they all need to have adequate reserves. You might have found that some tanks are low or even on empty. If this is the case, you might have to re-balance the time and effort you are putting in to individual tanks.

This was Frances' situation. Frances came to see me because she felt her life lacked 'fizz', as she called it. Indeed, it did – but perhaps she was closer to depression than simply being fizz-less. She certainly lacked a sense of life satisfaction. Frances was a thin woman with a noticeable lack of padding on her. She had never worked but had been very active as a mother and volunteer while her children were growing up. As a good corporate wife, she had kept the home fires burning while her husband worked and was always welcoming of the people he brought home for dinner. Her husband was successful and her children went to private schools. Frances had grown up in a family where there was little money and so further education was not available. I was surprised to learn this as Frances seemed to me to have the quintessential old money presentation. She reluctantly shared with me that she worked as a clerical assistant until her marriage. It was her reluctance to disclose this that alerted me to the importance of the information.

I asked Frances to complete the seven tanks exercise. Her physical tank was at 90 percent, intellectual at 30 percent, and social at 40 percent. Creativity and spirituality were virtually empty. Wellbeing was down to 15 percent. I asked Frances to help me understand why her physical tank was so high. She talked about how going to the gym, having a trainer, and keeping fit and slender (thin!) was something she could do and succeed at. It also meant that others envied her, and it made her feel better about her life and herself. The two pieces of information that stood out were her reluctance to disclose her origins and her need to feel better about herself. Her appearance was very high on her must-do list in order to feel emotionally safe. After a number of difficult conversations, Frances revealed that she had never felt she belonged in her husband's or children's world. She was the kid from the other side of the tracks who had made good and she felt like a fraud in her own life. She was still pouring all her energy into looking right and it was deadening.

The one thing approach

I suggested to Frances that she start to borrow some time from her fitness regime to begin to fill the other tanks. I asked her the question I am now going to ask you. What is *one thing* you can do to increase the fuel in each tank that is low? And if you are like Frances and putting too much into one or two tanks, what *one thing* can you do to reduce the energy you are putting in to a particular tank?

At first Frances was resistant. She did not want to change her bruising fitness schedule. However, she was prepared to do *one thing*. She agreed to reduce her treadmill session by 20 minutes and to use that 20 minutes to fill another tank. The tank she prioritised was creativity. She felt that having fuel in this tank would make the most difference. She had made many of her own clothes before she got married. She wondered if she might still have those skills. She decided to make an item of clothing for her only granddaughter, even though this child did not need to have clothes made for her as her parents were financially very comfortable (something Frances needed to tell me). This simple undertaking has changed Frances's life. She has found real joy in dressmaking. When her granddaughter's sartorial needs were met Frances decided to make children's clothes to donate for sale in charity shops. This began to fill her giving tank and her heart.

But we did not stop there. The wellbeing tank was her next target. Frances readily identified that she needed to take a risk and to stop trying to hide behind her well-constructed image. The *one thing* Frances undertook in order to fill her wellbeing tank was to ask at a market stall if she might provide handmade children's garments. Doing this took real courage as

Frances had always feared being seen as needy. For her, wealthy women did not trail around markets selling their wares. However, she did find an outlet for her garments and now she has a very small business. You can guess the *one thing* she did to bump up her intellectual tank: she did a small business course. She had considered handing over her accounts to her only son who is an accountant. But then, knowing she had tanks to fill, Frances decided to learn what she needed for herself. Before this story unfolded in its entirety Frances was willing to take more time from her fitness schedule. Her success gave her confidence. With the extra time she began to meditate. She did this at a community centre where she met with other women each week. Shyly, Frances told me that her own snobbishness had kept her lonely for many years. By doing meditation she had filled both her spirituality and social tanks.

Frances committed to her *one thing* bit by bit. You can follow her lead, or you can do as Carl did and commit to *one thing* for each tank and start immediately. Carl's wife had died a year before he came to see me. Carl very quickly identified his tank levels and could easily think of *one thing* he might do to increase the levels which were low across all tanks. He decided to go for a walk each morning (physical), start reading again (wellbeing), buy a book on photography and learn how to use his camera (intellectual), join the table tennis association (social), take one photograph a day (creative), and to go back to his local church (spiritual). You can see how these might all overlap. For example, to go for a walk each morning may also fill the social and wellbeing tanks; to start reading again will also be intellectual; to buy a book on photography and learn how to use his camera will have an impact on his creativity and wellbeing; to join the table tennis association will have an effect on the physical and wellbeing tanks; taking one photograph a day also fills intellectual and wellbeing tanks; and going back to his local church also impacts his social and wellbeing.

TASK: Balancing your tanks

Pull out the tanks you drew before. Write in each of your tanks ONE THING that you can do that will increase (or decrease if necessary, to give you more time) the level in that tank.

REFLECTION

Where will you start? Will one of your listed ONE THINGs fill more than one tank? If so, this might be a good place to start!

Life satisfaction is a critical part of a successful and satisfying retirement. Remember there is no should, no wrong or right, no pass or fail. What works for you and what satisfies you will be different to what works for and what satisfies others. The challenge is not just to know and understand yourself, but to have the courage to make and live your own life. I can assure you it will lead not only to retirement satisfaction but to life satisfaction.

---

[i] Sapolsky, R. (2001). 'Depression, antidepressants and the shrinking hippocampus'. *Proceedings of the National Academy of Sciences of the United States of America, 98*(22), 12320-12322.

[ii] Ferrix, L.T., Williams, J.S., & Shen, C.L. (2007). 'The effect of acute exercise on serum brain-derived neurotrophic factor levels and cognitive function'. *Medicine & Science in Sports & Exercise, 39*(4), 728-734.

[iii] Enders, G. (2015). Gut: The inside story of our body's most under-rated organ. Germany: Greystone Books.

[iv] Tilvis, R.S., Laitala, V., Routasalo, P. E., & Pitkala, K.H. (2011). 'Suffering from loneliness indicates significant mortality risk of older people'. *Journal of Aging Research,* Article ID: 534781, doi: https://doi.org/10.4061/2011/534781.

[v] Post, S.G. (2011). 'It's good to be good: 2011 fifth annual scientific report on health, happiness and helping others'. *International Journal of Person Centered Medicine, (1)*4. Retrieved from http://www.ijpcm.org/index.php/IJPCM/article/view/154.

[vi] http://worldhappiness.report/wp-content/uploads/sites/2/2015/04/WHR-2015-summary_final.pdf.

[vii] Australian Bureau of Statistics. (2014). *4159.0 – General social survey: Summary results, Australia, 2014*. Retrieved from: https://www.abs.gov.au/ausstats/abs@.nsf/mf/4159.0.

[viii] Izzo, J. B. (2008). *The five secrets you must discover before you die*. San Francisco: Berrett-Koehler Publishers, Inc.

[ix] Inagaki, T.K., Bryne Haltom, K,E., Suzuki, S., Jevtic, I., Hornstein, E., Bower, J.E., & Eisenberger, N.I. (2016). 'Receiving support: The role of stress-related and social reward-related neural activity'. *Psychosomatic Medicine, 78*(4), 443-453.

Chapter 20.

Resizing and relocating: Which way to go?

Downsizing, moving house, having a sea or tree change: often these are some of the big decisions of retirement. Of course, these decisions are not ones that are automatically part of retiring, but they do seem to come at about this time. Change begets change. Do you remember when you or your friends had a first baby? How many people, at about that time, decided to move house, remodel their current house, paint the house, re-stump it, or put in a new kitchen or a shed? It seems that we have it in our make up to create nests and then to change the nest to mark life changes and signify a new start. Some people signify retirement by going on a major holiday. But often, on their return, the downsizing and/or clearing process begins – planned or not. The clearing process is another activity that seems programmed to happen as we age, or when a life transition is happening. Many people will undertake a major clearing out of the contents of the home, even if they are not intending to move. Most people seem to find this almost cathartic rather than sad. They hire a skip, buy big black plastic bags, and set to work.

But there is also a group of people who avoid any change. They do not want to get rid of a thing, stoically stating that the only way they will leave their home is when they are carried out feet first, and that their lifetime of accumulated possessions will no longer be their problem. Take careful note, as you may find the instinct to mark a transition popping out in another way. For example, some people find they may need to buy a car: perhaps a smaller one OR a faster one!

What about you? Do you have things just as you want them, or will there be a change in your living arrangements in your retirement? Perhaps you shudder at the very thought of making a change?

Are you tempted to:

- leave your current home
- downsize your home
- move to a new locality
- downsize your possessions?

What do you need or want to do and how will you decide? What if your spouse thinks or feels differently? Let's have a look at each of the options above and discuss how to make these decisions.

To leave or to stay

Following is a list of statements that I have heard from people who are considering leaving their current their home:

- It is too big for us now.
- It is too hard to maintain, or it will be too hard in the future.
- It is too hard to leave the garden for long periods.
- If something happens to my husband/wife, I don't want to be left with the house to care for.
- It's time to move on. The current house has served its purpose.
- I want to live in a different sort of place … beach, bush, city.
- I want to live in a different sort of dwelling … unit, caravan, house, townhouse, cottage.
- If I sell this place, I can buy something smaller and have money left over to live on or invest.

- I want to move closer to the children or to a place that they might visit … like the beach.
- All of our friends have moved on.
- I want to be closer to services.
- We want to be closer to entertainment and restaurants.

The next list is of statements I have heard from people who are considering keeping the current home:

- I can't sell the kids' home. They would be devastated.
- We cannot agree on what we want.
- It is too hard to think about what we would have to do with all our possessions.
- I have so many possessions I wouldn't fit anywhere else.
- It is too hard to start again.
- The kids are not really settled. They might need to have a place to live again.
- We want to have enough space for the family to all come home for special occasions like Christmas and for family get togethers.
- We could never afford to replace what we have here.
- I know our neighbours and my local doctor etc.

There are good reasons for staying and good reasons for selling up. If you are not careful you can get caught in a cycle of argument. Similarly, you can get caught in a whirl of excitement and change.

Making the decision

Perhaps the most important part of this decision is to understand why you are considering leaving your home or why you do not want to leave. As you have read above, there are usually multiple factors to consider. There will be many underlying and contributing reasons and most people get lost in the pros and cons. If the pros and cons were decisive then the decision would be clear. You can reach clarity more easily through the process of identifying the priority reasons.

TASK: Deciding whether or not to move from your current home

Make your own lists of reasons why you want to leave and why you want to stay. Once you have done this, try and pick the one most important reason from both lists. This will be the priority reason for leaving and the priority reason for staying. Be aware that often the best reasons are not fact, but rather guesses of what might happen if you follow a course of action.

My top reason for leaving is: ....

....

My top reason for staying is: ....

....

REFLECTION

You have identified your top reason for leaving and your top reason for staying. Without considering all the other pros and cons, ask yourself, is the reason for staying or the reason for leaving more important? Which potential outcome do you want more?

When I compare my reason for leaving with my reason for staying and consider the likely outcome of each, I find that:

I value...more highly.

And I choose...

If you are part of a couple, do this task separately and then share your findings. Try to avoid the many paths into discussing other related factors until you complete this comparison of the two major reasons for staying and leaving.

Elsie and Bernard did the task. Bernard's lists were short and it was easy for him to identify the two top reasons. His top reason for leaving was because he had never lived at the beach and he had always wanted to try it. His top reason for staying was the effort involved in selling up and moving. Bernard quickly decided that the more important reason was to experience beach living. His decision was to move.

Elsie had a long list of reasons for staying and a long list for moving. Finally, she chose her top reason for selling and moving. She wanted to move to be nearer to her only child (who lived nowhere near a beach). Her top reason for staying was her role in the local historical society. Elsie struggled to identify which she wanted most; to be near to her son or to maintain her role in the history group. While she was struggling with the decision, Elsie realised she had failed to identify one of her reasons for moving. She wanted to move to support Bernard's long-held desire to experience beach living. This was more important to her than moving to be near her son or staying in the historical society. Together, Bernard and Elsie decided to rent out their house very cheaply to a family friend and to rent at the beach for six months.

The last time I saw them they had returned to their home and were very glad to leave the beach after the six-month trial. The trial had been a win-win for them. Bernard had enjoyed his experience but was glad to move home. Elsie felt content that she had supported Bernard. Her son had accepted a transfer elsewhere, so she was pleased they had not made a decision based on his place of living. They finally decided to buy a van and do long trips away rather than selling up and moving.

Downsizing your home

Downsizing is frequently a factor in the decision to move out of the current home. You may want to stay in the same geographical area but in a smaller or lower-maintenance abode.

TASK: Deciding whether to down-size your home

Use the same process described in the previous task to complete this task. Make lists of reasons why you want to downsize and why you do not want to downsize. Once you have done this, try and pick the one most important reason from both lists. This will be the priority reason for downsizing and the priority reason for not downsizing.

My top reason for downsizing is: ……………………………….....

……...……………………………………………………….....

My top reason for not downsizing is: ………………………….....

……………………………………………………………….......

REFLECTION

You have identified your top reason for downsizing and your top reason for not downsizing. Without considering all the other pros and cons, ask yourself whether the reason for downsizing or the reason for not downsizing is more important to you? Which potential outcome do you want more?

When I compare my reason for downsizing with my reason for not downsizing and consider the likely outcome of each, I find that:

I value…………………………………………………….more highly.

And I choose………………………………………………………....

If you are part of a couple, do this task separately and then share your findings. Try to avoid the many paths into discussing other related factors until you complete this comparison of the two major reasons for downsizing or not.

Harriet and Pat came to see me when they were considering selling their family home in order to downsize. They wanted to stay in the same locality. Would they go through the effort and disruption of selling just to live in a smaller home with a smaller garden? Harriet continued to raise the subject of downsizing because she wanted to avoid being left to care for their rambling house and large garden if Pat died suddenly. Pat felt that this was not an adequate reason to scale down and continued to try and assure her that, if he died, she could simply sell and move anytime. After arguments and tears, the result was a stalemate.

I asked Harriet and Pat to complete the downsizing task outlined earlier. Through this process, Harriet realised her top reason for downsizing was not, as she originally thought, to avoid being left with a large house and garden to maintain, but to avoid anxiety. Forty years ago, Harriet's father had died suddenly, leaving her mother with a 1,500-acre property to run on her own. The impact on Harriet's life had been profound and merely recalling that time made her feel anxious.

When Harriet had to identify her top reason for not downsizing, she struggled. She had been so invested in her ongoing argument with Pat about the need to downsize that she had not realised that she had some good reasons for not wanting to downsize. Her top reason was that her adult children and her grandchildren loved the house and the extensive gardens. Pat identified that he did not want to sell because he knew that their children saw the house as home and were proud of it. But he was tired of the maintenance of the house and gardens.

When they shared their findings, Harriet and Pat realised that they both wanted to leave for a similar reason. Pat was tired of maintenance and Harriet was anxious about becoming responsible for that maintenance. They wanted to stay for the same reason. They both believed the house was home for their adult children and that they felt responsible for providing a home. They were reluctant to take it away from their children, and while they each wanted to be free of the maintenance work/anxiety, they both felt unable to put their own wants above providing for their family.

A month later Pat and Harriet went to stay with their daughter Caroline and her husband Matt for a weekend visit. The house was quite simple but nestled in a secluded wooded area. In the car, after the visit to their daughter's home, Pat said to Harriet, 'Can you imagine Caroline saying to Matt that they cannot sell their house because Mum and Dad love coming here and see it as a real home away from home where they can relax?' Harriet smiled, 'Of course not. And anyway, they need to make decisions for their own little family, not for what they think we might need'. It was then that they looked at each other and it all fell into place. Well, not all of it fell into place, because they then had to decide where they wanted to move to and what sort of place they wanted to live in.

Deciding where to move to and what to live in

You have decided to move. The world is your oyster. Take out a map and decide where you want to live. Or perhaps it is not so simple and perhaps there are considerations and constraints on you. There are on most people. You may have elderly parents or young grandchildren to care for. You may not have enough money to make the choice you wish to make. In some ways having constraints makes decisions easier. The world is a big place and it can be hard to guess where to go to try your luck.

Beware of choosing a place to move to because you loved being there when on holidays. Holidays are a very different experience from day-to-day living. Holiday places are often just that ... a great place for a holiday. The happy experiences and memories that you have of that locality may be due more to the holiday feeling, and the activity or lack thereof, which takes place when you are holidaying. When making a decision about moving to a new location it is well worth asking people for their experiences. Of course, what happens for another person may not be relevant to you, but, as you listen, imagine yourself in that experience and how it might feel to you. How might it be different or similar?

Norma was very hurt when, on her retirement, she moved to the beach to be close to old friends and extended family. She had visited this town once a year and loved the warm welcome she received on her week-long annual visit. However, when she became just another resident, the parties and get togethers that she remembered from her annual holidays, and that she had imagined as being a part of her new life, did not happen. She had moved, not because she loved the beach, but for an existing social network. She did ask a few people about beach living. All said that they had to replace white goods frequently because of rust, and that home maintenance was costlier because of salt-induced rusting. Norma decided that, as everyone else could deal with this, she could too. However, the property prices at the beach were higher than the regional town she was leaving. Moving to the beach left her with reduced financial resources. Rust became a daily concern (if not an obsession) where Norma was constantly battling to wipe down white goods and to keep out the sea breeze.

Below is a list of criteria to consider when deciding where you want to live and what you want to live in.

Density
- City
- Regional town
- Village
- Rural
- Remote
- Beach

Type of dwelling
- House
- Cottage
- Townhouse
- Unit
- Gated community
- Retirement village
- Caravan/ motor home

Environment
- Land
- Acreage
- Garden
- Pots and plot
- On the ground
- Off the ground
- In a building complex
- Light and sunlight

Other factors

- Public transport options
- Health care facilities
- Traffic
- Climate – don't forget to consider humidity
- Culture, entertainment and restaurants
- Crime/security
- Affordability
- Cost of living. It is important that your income is about as high as the median for the area
- Creative outlets
- Proximity and accessibility to family and friends
- Access to like-minded people
- Service groups

TASK: Identifying where you would like to live and what sort of dwelling you would like to live in.

Create three vertical columns. In the first column on the left side of the page, list all the options and factors that are relevant and important to you. In the second column rate from 1 to 10 how important each option or factor is to you. When you find a potential new location in which to live, use the third column to rate out of 10 how well each option or factor is met. If you are considering more than one property just add another column for each.

REFLECTION

This will provide a quick snapshot of each housing option. If you are part of a couple complete the task individually and use it for comparison and discussion. You can also try assessing your current home using this method by adding extra columns.

Bronwyn knew the locality in which she wanted to live, but she was unsure if she wanted a house or unit. She had found a house to consider and a nice unit in the right area.

Factor	Importance	Factor match for 34 Bluebell St (House)	Factor match for 2/18 Dent St (Unit)
Walk to public transport	9	10	8
No mowing	7	0	10
Small garden	9	10	2
Quiet area	5	8	8
No stairs	4	10	3

When Bronwyn reflected on her scores, she realised that having access to the garden was more important to her than the mowing she had hoped to avoid.

Downsizing your possessions without downsizing your house

Downsizing your house forces you to downsize your possessions. But it is possible to downsize your possessions without moving house. Sometimes downsizing of possessions is all that you need to do and the need to move house seems to disappear. It is well worth ruthlessly getting rid of the stuff you have accumulated in your house as though you were moving to a smaller abode and then seeing what happens. If you still want to move, your thoughts will be clearer as will your awareness of how much space you really need.

It is hard to let go of possessions. It is hard because it is hard to believe that the sentimental value placed on items has no real value. Once the item has been discarded it is somewhat startling to realise how easy it is to let it go. The main thing is to start. Try not to work with anyone else as you may find that you spend more time talking about whether or not to keep something rather than moving stuff on. However, if you are struggling to make a start, bring in a friend who is not sentimental and who can keep you on track. It is not just sentimental items that might trip you up but the thought that, 'I might need this again sometime'. The likelihood is that there is now a better version of the same thing that is easily available should you need it.

Your possessions: an inheritance or a source of family conflict?

Think twice about gifting possessions that you no longer want. Admittedly, it makes it much easier to discard an item that you have valued if you believe it is going to someone else who will value it. It is like keeping the item but getting someone else to care for it. It usually means that you have not completely separated yourself from the item. What will happen if the person does not care for it in the way that you think is appropriate, or if the person sells it or even throws it out? This happens repeatedly when parents hand over possessions to their adult children. It can cause conflict and hurt.

So how do you dispose of possessions that you believe have worth? Who decides if those possessions are worthwhile? I have heard a variety of stories telling of different approaches. Let me share with you the keys that seem to lead to success.

The keys

1. Recipient identification.
2. Inclusiveness.
3. Timing.

Firstly, identify who the primary group of recipients should be. For example, they could be your adult children or your grandchildren or your siblings. Secondly, act with inclusiveness. I do not mean to include everyone you can think of but include the recipients in your thinking. Let them know what you are planning and what you want to achieve. For example, you might tell them that you are planning to disperse your possessions. You want to achieve a fair distribution. You do not want to put anyone under pressure to take anything more than that which they may want. Nor do you want anyone to take anything except what they want for themselves rather than for others. You want everyone to be honest in what they would like even if their desires seem greedy. It does not mean that they will get it. It is a time for honesty. It is not a time to harbour or create new resentments. The possessions are yours and you will decide. Thirdly, timing – make sure you send the message to everyone at the same time.

Four years ago, Bob's wife died. He had stayed on in their home as he did not want to rush into making changes that he might regret. Finally, he decided to move into a retirement complex. He had four adult children and he kept them informed of his plans as those plans developed. His two daughters encouraged Bob to start getting rid of possessions as soon as he started to talk about moving. His older daughter had always had an eye for what she wanted and started to drop comments about things that she had fondness for and would like to have. His younger daughter was more interested in everyone getting the same amount. Neither of the boys were interested and both said that it looked like a heap of rubbish to them.

Once Bob had sorted out what he wanted to take with him to his new home he wrote an email to his children. In it, he said that he had a collection of possessions for distribution. He invited everyone to come at any time and put their name on anything that they wanted to take. If there was more than one name on any item, those people could come to an arrangement or a name would be drawn out of a hat. Everything was to be left in place in four (one per child) observable heaps until a nominated pick up day. After that time, he was inviting the grandchildren to pick what they wanted with the same rules and for a Skype session for the ones who lived out of town. Once the date passed for the grandchildren to choose and then collect their things, he would ring St Vincent de Paul.

Bob reported that it went well. His older daughter had a large heap of things that she wanted, which surprised no-one. The younger daughter had a smaller heap but with some more valuable pieces that she had traded for with her sister. Neither boy had shown much interest until it came to Bob's tools. He did not allow the children's spouses to come in to the house to be a part of the process.

In Bob's situation, his children wanted some of his possessions. This is not always the case. Be careful of trying to persuade someone to take what you think they might need or should have.

Joanne's grandmother had given her daughter (Joanne's mother) a large, and somewhat ugly, heavy wooden tray that she had carved herself when she was quite young. Joanne's mother had never liked it, but she felt a loyalty to her mother that would not let her throw it out. She was only too happy to give the tray to Joanne when Joanne moved into her first home and had few possessions. Joanne's mother felt she could finally rid herself of the tray in an honourable way. Joanne, granddaughter of the tray maker, is now in her 50s and feels she is stuck with the tray. How can she throw it out? How can she burden her own daughter with it? Using the second key of inclusiveness, my 50-year-old friend told her daughter of her dilemma and of her decision to throw out the tray unless her daughter had another opinion. To her surprise, her daughter said that she had always loved the tray and wanted to make it into a wall hanging. Remember the old adage, one person's treasure is another person's trash and vice versa.

A book that addresses decluttering and downsizing of possessions is *The life-changing magic of tidying: A simple, effective way to banish clutter forever* by Marie Kondo.[i] In it, she has a section on how to identify what is truly precious. She says that when a person is faced with a decision of whether to keep or discard something, the person will pause and frown just a little, which indicates that the item that should not be kept. If the item is truly precious to the person there will be no frown and no hesitation as the decision is usually instantaneous.

Once you have downsized a lifetime of possessions into a collection of items you truly value and regularly use, you will find that there is more space around you. In the new space you may find that you will be able to breathe more easily and move more freely. In your altered space you may no longer feel the need to sell up.

Another thought

One common reason for selling and moving house is to free up money. The idea is that if you sell your current home and buy something smaller, then you will have money left over which can be used to support your lifestyle. I am highlighting this reason as it needs careful consideration. It is not always the case that you will come away with cash in the hand. There are many costs to selling and buying a dwelling. You may find that the process of selling your house and buying another will cost you a significant amount of money. Make sure you talk in detail to a real estate agent about fees and costs for selling, and fees and costs for buying. Talk to the bank and to the holder of your mortgage, if you have one, about fees and costs.

---

[i] Kondo, M. (2014). The life-changing magic of tidying: A simple, effective way to banish clutter forever. London: Vermilion.

Chapter 21.

Grandparenting:
Your next job?

It seems that many people are moving into retirement only to find themselves working in a new, but unpaid, job. Your emotions and your value system might drive you to participate in this work. Guilt and a sense of responsibility are often part of the equation, as are love and care and joy. In this job the hours can be exhausting and involve shift work. There is no overtime or time-and-a-half. Your boss can be irrational, cry, and throw tantrums. Your supervisor will want a report at the end of each shift. But, on the other hand, your little boss will kiss you and hug you and be a joy to watch. Hopefully your supervisor will be grateful and appreciative and be willing to learn from your experience. Being the carer to your grandchildren is an onerous, but rewarding, job.

Child care has become unaffordable for many. Paying for child care can make working for financial gain a pointless exercise. The pressure is on the grandparents to step in and provide a child care service so that parents can return to work and make money.

Are you up to the job?

If you are asked to provide child care, how do you decide if you are physically, emotionally, and mentally fit to undertake the role? Having sole responsibility for a child is a lot of work, and stressful. There will be more stress and pressure in caring for someone else's child than there was in caring for your own. If possible, it is always a good idea to start small and build up. It may sound easy to do one day a week, but that day can be exhausting and seem endless. Over time a child will get bigger and therefore harder to hold, lift, and restrain. And as that child is getting bigger, stronger and heavier you are probably getting smaller and weaker! So, start small. Perhaps a few hours a week. Build in a review before care arrangements begin and plan to have scheduled reviews thereafter.

Sometimes, when the parent is presented with a job offer or similar opportunity, there will be pressure to start full-time or a full day or two immediately. To prevent this, try and initiate an anticipatory conversation with the parent. Ask if you will be wanted to provide any child care in the future. And if the answer is yes, suggest that you start with a small regular commitment to trial it. The trial must be from your perspective, from that of the parent, and from the child's or children's. You may have already been doing bits and pieces of child care, but it is different when it is a scheduled commitment.

TASK: Negotiating the job parameters

If you have accepted the job of providing child care, it will be important to work out limits before you start the job. Try answering the following questions:

- *Will you provide care in your home or in the child's home?*
- *How many days are you willing to work and for how many hours?*
- *Are you prepared to have change at short notice?*
- *Are you providing food and nappies etc. or are they being sent with the child?*
- *Who will provide the cot, high chair, baby monitor etc.?*
- *Are you able to drive the child or children?*
- *Can the child or children go with you to visit your friends or to your activities?*
- *Are you able to discipline your way?*
- *Who determines the structure (sleep times etc.) of the day?*

- *Are you allowed to decide about the use of a dummy?*
- *Are you allowed to decide whether or not to let the child cry?*
- *Are you allowed to give the child a bottle or a cup as you see fit?*
- *Who will decide the food rules?*
- *Are you able to provide treats and toys?*
- *Who decides about the use of electronic screens including TV/games/internet/phones?*
- *How do you get a rest or time to yourself during the day, and/or an opportunity to do your own jobs?*
- *How will you talk about problems and concerns which arise?*

REFLECTION

Is there anything that you need to discuss with the child's parents? It is better to have difficult conversations before problems arise than when the situation has deteriorated.

Your life

Many grandparents seem to find that they are very successful at providing child care ... so successful that before long they are being asked to extend their hours. This can be very difficult. You love your child and want to help. You love your grandchild and want to be a part of his or her life. But you need to maintain your own life.

Simone gave willingly of her time to care for her three grandchildren. She started when they were babies and then, as they got older, she loved taking them to kindy and to school. When she had one at school, one in kindy, and one at home, her son got a job in the UK. It was a mad, exciting rush to get them to the UK. Simone even went with them to help on the journey. When she returned, she found she did not have a life of her own, friends of her own or activities of her own.

It is essential to keep your own life ticking over. Some grandparents have had to let go of their retirement expectations to assume the role of full-time care givers in order to protect the children from their parents. It is very hard to maintain your independence in this situation and I would encourage you to seek support from others and from services.

Saying NO

In order to keep some of your life for yourself you might have to say no to people you love. How do you say this difficult word? I strongly encourage you not to say yes if you want to say no. Whenever you are asked a question to which you might wish to answer no, but feel uncomfortable in doing so, try to pause. There are very few times when it is necessary to answer on the spot. Simply ask for time to think about it. Then you will have time to formulate your response.

When Jillian was asked to provide some care for her grandson, she asked for time to think about it. After she considered how she would respond, she said to her son and daughter-in-law, 'Thank you for giving me the opportunity to be involved in caring for Addison. I have had to really think about it as I did not want to say yes and then let you down or feel resentful; that would not be fair to you or Addison. I love being with Addi, but I am going to say no. I know this puts you under more pressure to find someone to provide care and it will be more expensive, but I can't do it for you'. You will note that Jillian did not offer reasons. However, her daughter-in-law did not hesitate to ask her why she would not do it. Jillian said, 'I have a number of reasons, some of which I will not share with you and some that I will. I retired only eight months ago. I have not yet had my time to find my feet and learn how to be retired or to discover who I want to be and what I want to do. I do not want to be committed; just as you do want to be committed and able to go to work. We are in the same place but going in opposite directions. I hope at some stage in the future I will be able to be here for you and to help with Addison or the next baby, but that time is not now'. Jillian told me that her son was accepting of her decision but that her daughter-in-law was resentful for some time, until she realised that Jillian was still going to provide some babysitting at night when they wanted to go out.

The rules for saying 'no' are to pause and think. Take as long as you need. Then, when you respond, offer some thanks. Often being asked to do more is a mark of trust and appreciation of the good job that you are currently doing. When you say no, keep it short. Keep it clear. No has to be no. Not, 'I don't think …'. Saying, 'I am not sure', or, 'I don't think', will lead to questions and to your being encouraged or pressured, because if you are not sure then maybe you can be persuaded. You do not have to offer reasons or justifications.

Tricks and traps

There are a couple of tricks to watch out for when you are negotiating the limit of your involvement. People use these strategies unconsciously. Your family is not trying to manipulate you, but they will be trying to get what they want … which is normal. Unless you are aware of it, you may find yourself agreeing despite your best intentions.

The hook

An example of a request which uses guilt as a hook is as follows: 'I just don't know how little Sammy will go in child care. He loves you and he is used to being at home with you. I think he is too young to go to a centre, all those germs! But I guess he will have to go if you can't do it'. Don't respond to hooks that are thrown out in the hope of catching you. Simply repeat your decision kindly and respectfully. Guilt is a poor reason for any action.

The A-B sequence trap

This is how the A-B sequence trap works. You are asked for A. In this situation, A might be a request to do two extra days of child care. 'Mum, would you be able to do another two days of looking after Sammy? I have been offered extra work. I don't know how long it is for, but it would be fantastic if I could grab the work while it is going. We really need the money. And I don't want to put Sammy into care if it turns out to be only for a few weeks.' You respond with (a carefully worded) no.

Next you are asked for B. B will be something less than A. 'Well, Mum, what if you just did it for four weeks and by then I should know whether the work will continue or not.' Most people struggle to say no, so that when the next request comes and it is lesser, the temptation is to say yes.

The give-give sequence trap

In the give-give sequence you give me something before you ask me for something. I will be more likely to respond positively, because we naturally reciprocate. You smile, I smile. You frown, I frown. You give, I give. Your toddling grandson comes in with a clumsily wrapped gift for you and a card attached saying, 'Thank you, Pa, for looking after me every Wednesday. I love being with you. Will you look after me on Tuesday too?'

Money

It is not unusual for grandparents to go into retirement in order to provide child care. If you do this, you will need to do some careful work on evaluating your financial position. Can you afford it? Are you going to be compensated financially by the parents you are assisting? You may have to bring it up if they do not offer. Even a small contribution can make a difference when you no longer have money coming in. Perhaps there can be a payment-in-kind arrangement if the parent is unable to pay you. In one family I know, the parents of the two grandchildren cooked each weekend and made dinners for the week ahead. Instead of money they sent three frozen dinners each week to the grandparents, along with the children.

If you are providing full-time care you may be eligible for financial assistance from the government. This is worth exploring.

Variations

So far, we have looked at a couple of scenarios of grand-parenting arrangements. It is unrealistic to think that that there is a typical arrangement. Your situation is unlikely to be the same as others. All families are different with different dynamics and histories.

Waiting in the wings

I want to acknowledge those who are waiting with dwindling hope of becoming grandparents. There can be great sadness in this situation. Your time is free, but your arms are empty. This might be because your children have not produced offspring or because you have not been invited into your grandchildren's lives. It is a pain that can be similar to that of parents who are unable to conceive. You might grieve the loss of a role to which you had looked forward and had expected would be part of your life. You might find yourself separated from your peers in conversation and activity as they share their grandparenting stories. This situation presents a challenge to your identity and you may find it helpful to re-read the chapter on identity and focus on reinventing yours.

Rejection

You may be very keen to provide the care for your grandchildren but not be invited to do so. One grandmother was devastated when her daughter-in-law anxiously told her that they did not trust her to be alone with the children, because she tended to drop things and they thought her driving was not safe.

Safety

Some grandparents have had to let go of their retirement expectations to assume the role of full-time care givers in order to protect the children from their parents. This may be due to a variety of issues including drugs or alcohol, violence and abuse, and/or a severe mental health disorder.

Caring for adolescents

It is regularly assumed that the care-giving will be to a baby, toddler or young child. Yet many grandparents are caring for adolescents. I have seen these families in my practice as they strive to live well together. Sometimes the adolescents have requested that they live with the grandparents. Again, there have been a variety of reasons. One could not tolerate her stepfather. One lived in a remote area and was not coping at boarding school. Another was becoming a young star in his sport and was wanting to attend competitions plus training. His grandparents lived close to the action while his parents lived some distance away. If you are going to provide a home for adolescents, then it is very important to establish the rules in conjunction with that child and his or her parents. Make sure that the school knows who you are, and that you have authority with the school.

TASK: Negotiating the job parameters

If you have accepted the job of providing care for an older child or adolescent it will be important to work out limits before you start the job. Try answering the following questions:

- *Who is providing food, clothing, transport, pocket money, incidentals?*
- *Will you be provided with a cash kitty in order to supplement as necessary?*
- *Do you have a say in what the adolescent can do outside of school hours?*
- *Do you have a say in where the adolescent can go outside of school times and with whom?*
- *Who decides and pays for mobile phone use?*
- *Who decides on rules for use of screens?*
- *Who decides about bedtime and curfew limits?*
- *Who decides who can be in the adolescent's room and how the room is used?*
- *Do you have a say in what the adolescent eats?*
- *Is alcohol permitted?*
- *Are you allowed to discipline your way?*
- *What are your house rules that you would like to have followed?*

REFLECTION

There are many more parameters to negotiate. And many more questions and concerns will come up during the course of your time together, so it is important to have a way of discussing and navigating these as they arise. Build in a regular review time that includes the adolescent and the parent/s. If the parent/s are not in-volved, then make the review arrangement with the adolescent.

A quote from a grandfather:

When my wife and I started to provide some help to our kids by looking after their kids, it was only two mornings per week. It was quite good fun. In fact, I used to look forward to it. I had been retired for about a year and I was starting to struggle with the time on my hands and I was feeling a bit purposeless. The kids were fun (more fun than my wife) and then they went home. So, when we were asked to do more, I did not have a problem with it. We did not talk about the limits, we just started to do whatever was asked of us.

Our son is a nurse and does shift work. His wife is a teacher and she didn't want to go back to work full-time, but she wanted to do relief work. I think she liked it for the break from the kids as much as for the money. I envied her. I would have liked to have had a job that I could go to like that. Anyway, we just did as asked, and sometimes it gave me a bit of a shot in the arm when the phone would ring early and I would have to get organised fast and jump in the car to go and collect the kids.

But slowly it became more routine and I felt like I had a job that was eating away my opportunities to develop other parts of my life. That was hard. My wife and I would discuss it at length. Should we set limits, or should we just accept our role? She said that we were lucky to be such a big part of the lives of our kids and grandkids and if we started to set limits, we might lose them. She would say things like, 'How could we enjoy travelling around the country for months if we knew the kids were at home struggling?' I would think, 'Well, I could enjoy it, but if you can't it won't be much fun going on a trip together'. On the plus side, I really love those kids. I'm glad that they know me so well and that I know them so well. I don't think we will ever lose that connection. It has come at a cost, but it is one I have been prepared to pay. So, we just kept going. We are still going ...

Conclusion

Retirement is a precious opportunity. The cohort of people reaching retirement age, with an expectation of a government funded or assisted retirement, is increasing rapidly. At the same time, we have entered a period of world economic turmoil and uncertainty. This unprecedented combination is fanning fear. It has led to fear of leaving work and stepping into retirement. Many people are unsure whether they can afford retirement and are unwilling to let go of their lifestyle. The result is an increasing focus on the financial aspects of retirement, perhaps at the expense of the psychological aspects. It is these psychological factors that you have been investigating as you worked your way through the book.

TASK: Completing the retirement audit again

Return to the retirement audit that you completed before reading this book. You will find it in the Introduction. Complete it again and see what has changed.

REFLECTION

Have you made satisfactory progress on all factors or on those important to you? Do you need to review particular chapters?

'Your life does not get better by chance. It gets better by change.'
— Jim Rohan

This book is about change: anticipating it, embracing it, planning for it. And retirement, like every other phase of life, will be full of change. Retirement is not a destination, despite the retirement cards full of well wishes indicating that you have arrived there. Unlike other life phases, where the changes are usually additions – a new course of study, a new job, a new spouse, a new baby – retirement changes are frequently about subtractions – not working, not earning, not having time constraints. Perhaps we have less experience in dealing with this type of passive change and are therefore less savvy in dealing with it. A good retirement is not just about surviving change, but of thriving through the opportunities that change provides. It is a time to invent and re-invent yourself, your identity, your purpose, and your occupation. Dr Robert Butler, in his 1975 Pulitzer winning book *Why survive? Being old in America*,[i] wrote that 'human beings need the freedom to live with change, to invent and reinvent themselves a number of times through their lives'. I hope that, newly armed with a wealth of information, skills, and self-knowledge, you feel empowered to respond to the changes brought by retirement. A quote often attributed to Charles Darwin is that, 'it is not the strongest of the species that survives, nor the most intelligent, but the one most responsive to change'.

And now it is time to complete a final task.

TASK: Reviewing your retirement vision

In Chapter 2: Starting with the end you began to create a vision of your retirement. Write about your vision as it is NOW, before turning back to Chapter 2 and reviewing your original response. Write from the heart, forget all the 'shoulds' and 'musts' and limitations that you believe you have. Think about what you have learned as you completed the tasks in this book. Let those learnings guide you.

REFLECTION

When you have honed your vision, perhaps make a statement of intent or create a diagram or picture about it. Where will you put this statement so that reading it or looking at your vision can become a part of your day? How often will you review both your vision and your performance? Put the review date in your diary.

If you believe that you have invested wisely by reading this book, then it is important that you maintain the value of your investment. To do this, I would again encourage you to keep your writings and responses to the tasks, so that you can access them in the future. At this stage, if you were my client and coming to see me in my rooms, I would ask you to return for a review. We would have a number of reviews some months apart. During the reviews we would look at what you have achieved and whether you are on track with your plans and implementing of change. We would redo the Satisfaction With Life Scale, from *Chapter 18: Happiness, life satisfaction, and wellbeing*. Our reviews would become annual check-ups where I might ask you to repeat some of the tasks that you did in the book and to notice how your responses have changed. I hope that you will undertake to review your progress. It may be helpful to work with a friend who has also read this book.

The challenge of retirement is to live its possibilities. What will you do to capture those possibilities and turn them into realities? I hope now you will be able to answer this question confidently. You have committed time and energy into acquiring a bank of information, a set of maps and a full tool box for navigating retirement. You have developed a vision, set a course, and honed your skills for moving through the uncharted waters of transition. Importantly, you have clarified and actioned the principles which promote life satisfaction and personal wellbeing. In short, you have acquired the skills that underpin the psychological requirements for achieving a successful and fulfilling retirement.

The last words belong to Sophia Loren, who remained a media favourite in her 80s, and to Socrates, who is considerably older and just as famous. Sophia Loren's words reflect some of your learnings from this book. She said, 'There is a fountain of youth: it is your mind, your talents, the creativity you bring to your life and the lives of people you love'.

Socrates, around 400 BC, chipped in with, 'The secret of change is to focus all of your energy, not on fighting the old, but on building the new'.

It is my hope that you follow Socrates's advice and build the new, using your talents and creativity together with your new knowledge, to create a retirement of which you will be proud. May you live your retirement your way and may it continue to sustain you like a long drink from the fountain of youth.

---

[i] Butler, R.N. (1975). *Why survive? Being old in America.* New York: Harper & Row.